CW00960343

CAMPAIGN 79

LOUISBOURG 1758

WOLFE'S FIRST SIEGE

SERIES EDITOR: LEE JOHNSON

CAMPAIGN 79

LOUISBOURG 1758

WOLFE'S FIRST SIEGE

WRITTEN BY
RENÉ CHARTRAND

BATTLESCENE PLATES BY
PATRICE COURCELLE

First published in Great Britain in 2000 by Osprey Publishing, Elms Court, Chapel Way, Botley, Oxford OX2 9LP United Kingdom
Email: info@ospreypublishing.com

© 2000 Osprey Publishing Ltd.

All rights reserved. Apart from any fair dealing for the purpose of private study, research, criticism or review, as permitted under the Copyright, Designs and Patents Act, 1988, no part of this publication may be reproduced, stored in a retrieval system, be transmitted in any form or by any means, electronic, electrical, chemical, mechanical, optical, photocopying, recording or otherwise, without the prior written permission of the copyright owner. Enquiries should be addressed to the Publisher.

ISBN 1 84176 217 2

Editor: Marcus Cowper
Design: Ken Vail Graphic Design, Cambridge, UK

Colour bird's-eye-view illustrations by the Black Spot
Cartography by Ken Vail Graphic Design, Cambridge, UK
Battlescene artwork by Patrice Courcelle
Originated by Valhaven, Isleworth, UK
Printed in China through World Print Ltd

00 01 02 03 04   10 9 8 7 6 5 4 3 2 1

For a Catalogue of all books published by Osprey Military
and Aviation please write to:
The Marketing Manager, Osprey Publishing Ltd., P.O. Box 140,
Wellingborough, Northants NN8 4ZA United Kingdom
Email: info@ospreydirect.co.uk

The Marketing Manager, Osprey Direct USA, P.O. Box 130,
Sterling Heights, MI 48311-0130, United States of America
Email: info@ospreydirectusa.com

Or visit Osprey at:
www.ospreypublishing.com

Dedication

To William and Helen O'Shea, my old friends and fellow scouts in Louisbourg, Nova Scotia.

Acknowledgments

Friend and fellow historian Donald E. Graves provided ideas and data as to the various stages of Louisbourg's last siege. The staff members at Fortress Louisbourg National Historic Site, at the National Archives of Canada (Ottawa), at the Library of the Canadian War Museum (Ottawa) and at the Library of the Department of Canadian Heritage (Hull) were most kind in providing efficient and timely assistance. Patrice Courcelle skillfully illustrated key events in the siege. Osprey editor Marcus Cowper turned it all into a handy and visually pleasing volume. To one and all, please accept my heartfelt expression of deepest gratitude.

Artist's Note

Readers may care to note that the original paintings from which the colour plates in this book were prepared are available for private sale. All reproduction copyright whatsoever is retained by the publisher. All enquiries should be addressed to:

Patrice Courcelle, 33 Avenue des Vallons, 1410 Waterloo, Belgium

The publishers regret that they can enter into no correspondence on this matter.

KEY TO MILITARY SYMBOLS

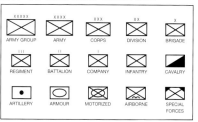

CONTENTS

Louis XV, king of France, who reigned from 1715 to 1774. (Print after Quentin de La Tour's 1746 portrait)

ORIGINS OF THE CAMPAIGN

LOUISBOURG: A MILITARY AND ECONOMIC STRONGHOLD

"Isle Royale protects all the French trade in North America, and is of no small consequence to the trade they conduct further south. If they [the French] had nothing in this part of the world, their ships which come back from Saint-Domingue [Haiti] or Martinique, would not be safe on the Grand Banks of Newfoundland, especially in times of war. Finally, being at the entrance of the gulf [of St Lawrence], she controls totally that river."

This description of the importance of Isle Royale (or Cape Breton Island) in the *Lettres et Mémoires* (1760) of Thomas Pichon sums up perfectly the strategic importance of Cape Breton Island during the reigns of Louis XV of France and George II of Great Britain. Louisbourg, the capital of the French colony of Isle Royale, took on a pivotal role in the great contest for the domination of North America: whoever controlled the island and the fortress of Louisbourg had the key to New France.

Cape Breton Island was known to European sailors from the turn of the 16th century, and some believe it was discovered by John Cabot. Certainly, English, French, Spanish and Portuguese sailors frequented the area, and in the 1520s a Portuguese colony was apparently attempted but it failed. There were subsequently a few modest, short-lived settlements. The European presence was basically seasonal as it was based on exploiting the fisheries. The first recorded European visit to what would become Louisbourg harbor was by the Englishman Captain Charles Leigh in the *Chancewell* on 7 July 1597. The place became known as Havre à L'Anglois (English Harbor).

The history of the French on Cape Breton Island is interlinked with that of the early French settlements in Acadia (which roughly encompassed western Nova Scotia and eastern New Brunswick) and Placentia (southern Newfoundland). The first French settlements were established by the French explorer Samuel de Champlain at Isle Sainte-Croix (near St Andrews, New Brunswick) in 1603. He moved on to build an enclosed "habitation" at Port Royal (near Annapolis Royal, Nova Scotia) in 1604, and founded Quebec in 1608. From that time small settlements were established in what the French called Acadia. Times were often turbulent for these settlers. The original Port Royal was destroyed in 1613 by English colonial privateers from Virginia, but the settlement was rebuilt nearby and prospered. Over the years, Acadia was subject to various attacks and invasions by New Englanders, and also suffered occasional civil strife. During the 1660s and 1670s, Louis XIV took some measures to consolidate the French positions in Acadia and installed a permanent station on the southern coast of Newfoundland to protect French interests in the Grand Bank fisheries. By the 1680s, permanent garrisons of colonial troops were being established, both in Acadia and Placentia, and ships going back and forth from Europe to North America and the West Indies made frequent stopovers.

The wars between the French and English during the 1690s and early 1700s brought much military activity to the area. Port Royal and Placentia were attacked several times, first by the New Englanders alone and, eventually, with help from Britain. For all that, the French gave as good as they got. The frontier of Maine was devastated by the Chevalier de Saint-Castin and his Abenakis and Micmac Indian allies; the English fishery stations in Newfoundland were devastated and St John's captured by the French. Eventually, Port Royal, the capital of Acadia, was captured by a large combined British and New England force in 1710 and renamed Annapolis Royal.

The Treaty of Utrecht, signed in 1713 between Britain and France, conceded Acadia (which confirmed it as Nova Scotia) and Newfoundland to Britain. France, however, kept Cape Breton Island and Isle Saint-Jean (the future Prince Edward Island). In July 1713, some 150 French colonists sailed from Placentia to Isle Royale, as Cape Breton Island was now rebaptized and resettled at the most likely harbor, Havre à L'Anglois, now renamed Port Saint-Louis. There were other settlements in the years to follow, notably at Port Toulouse (now St Peter's) and Port Dauphin (St Ann's), but in 1719, Port Saint-Louis was renamed Louisbourg and a fortress and naval base erected. They were inaugurated in 1720 and, for the next 23 years, a town surrounded by substantial fortifications rose.

Apparently, when presented with more bills to pay for Louisbourg's construction, Louis XV once said that he expected to see its spires from Versailles' windows. The story is, no doubt, apocryphal. For all the expenses recorded, it was only a small part of France's vast expenditure on works on dozens of other fortresses at the time. And even then, Louisbourg never had a real citadel. True, Louisbourg did not come

LEFT **The "Habitation" of Port Royal, built by Samuel de Champlain in 1604, was the nucleus to the French settlements on Canada's Atlantic coast, a presence which ended with the capture of Louisbourg in 1758. (Print after Champlain)**

RIGHT **Three medals marked *"Lusovicoburgum Fundatum et Munitum M DCC XX"* (Louisbourg founded and armed 1720) with the profile of young King Louis XV. They were found in the cornerstone of the King's Bastion, encased in a rectangle of leather-covered wood. (Fortress Louisbourg National Historic Site, Louisbourg, Nova Scotia)**

cheap, but on the other hand, it was a commercial success. It provided French Grand Banks fishermen with a secure harbor and their activities, which had been ruined during Queen Anne's War, were totally restored by 1718 and expanded thereafter. In spite of having a short season, Louisbourg's harbor became the scene of intense maritime traffic from France, Canada, the West Indies and the British 13 colonies – these last included a fair amount of smuggling.

TAKEN AND HANDED BACK

By the 1740s, the town had grown to about 4,000 souls and had, according to some accounts, become the fourth busiest harbor in North America. The New Englanders hated the outright competition, and one suspects the Bible-quoting volunteers who, almost incredibly, took Louisbourg in 1745, also wanted to appropriate this exceptionally good commercial port. The town's population was deported to France while Britain immediately posted a strong garrison there. France wanted Louisbourg back and in 1746, sent out a fleet under the Duke d'Anville carrying five battalions and a train of artillery. It was cursed by bad luck and dispersed by a hurricane. D'Anville and many men subsequently died of sickness and the remnants limped back to France.

By the 1748 Treaty of Aix-la-Chapelle, Fortress Louisbourg was returned to France. It seems the British wanted Madras (India) back as

BELOW **A view of Fortress Louisbourg in 1731. Less than a dozen years after its foundation, the town flourished and had achieved the general appearance it would keep until July 1758. (Print after Verrier)**

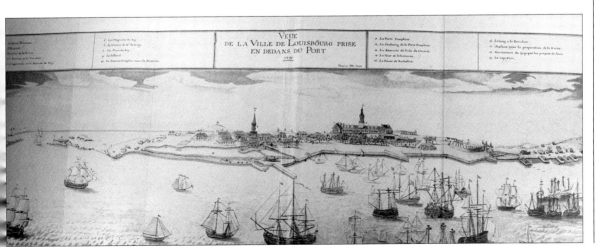

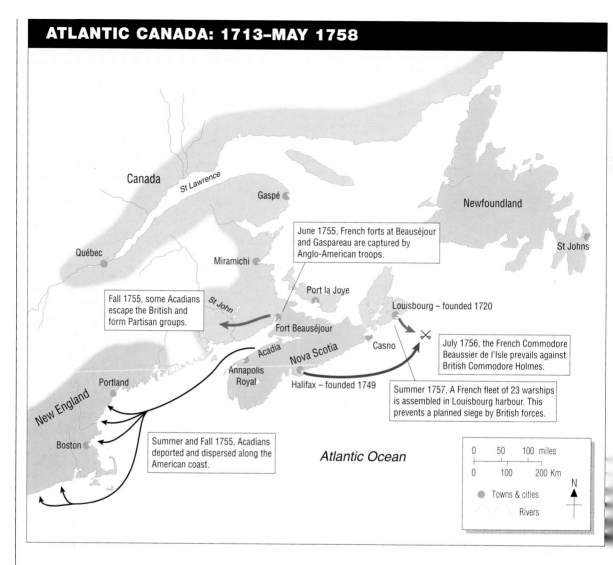

Canada

St Lawrence

Gaspé

Newfoundland

St Johns

June 1755, French forts at Beauséjour and Gaspareau are captured by Anglo-American troops.

Québec

Miramichi

Port la Joye

Louisbourg – founded 1720

Fall 1755, some Acadians escape the British and form Partisan groups.

St John

Fort Beauséjour

Acadia

Nova Scotia

Casno

July 1756, the French Commodore Beaussier de l'Isle prevails against British Commodore Holmes.

Annapolis Royal

Portland

Halifax – founded 1749

Summer 1757, A French fleet of 23 warships is assembled in Louisbourg harbour. This prevents a planned siege by British forces.

New England

Boston

Summer and Fall 1755, Acadians deported and dispersed along the American coast.

Atlantic Ocean

| 0 | 50 | 100 miles |
| 0 | 100 | 200 Km |

N

Towns & cities

Rivers

it had been captured by the French. Needless to say, the New Englanders were not amused and indeed quite bitter. This reaffirmed that Louisbourg was more than just a successful commercial port, it was a strategic naval base which could command the North Atlantic if a strong enough fleet was posted there. It was the sentry to Canada and its vast expanses deep into North America. The French doubled the garrison and, from then on, sizable French warships patrolled the waters around Isle Royale. However, Louisbourg's fortifications benefited from only summary repairs. The emphasis was on rebuilding trade and commerce and, within a few years, the town was flourishing again with a population of about 4,500 souls.

Although they seemed formidable, Louisbourg's fortifications had many defects. The masonry was crumbling in many of the existing works and needed repair. In 1754, Col. Franquet, a senior engineer, was sent to the fortress to improve it. His efforts were generally ineffective as the French government would not grant enough money. To be truly safe, the Royal Battery would require major defenses on its landward side. A strong fort should be built on Lighthouse Point to fully secure the

ABOVE RIGHT **The crenellated walls of the Dauphin Bastion.**

BELOW RIGHT **View of the gun platform inside the Dauphin Bastion, mounted with 24-pdr. cannon.**

harbor's entrance and prevent the Island Battery from being bombarded. The town's ramparts and bastions needed counterguards, ravelins and demi-lunes. Most of all, Louisbourg needed a citadel. Such a project seemed so hopeless insofar as official approval was concerned that the engineers did not even propose plans they knew would be rejected. The British called the King's Bastion the "Citadel" but it was merely a big bastion. Louisbourg did not have a proper citadel, the ultimate stronghold found in most fortified cities. Thus, in the event of heavy bombardments or of a breach followed by an assault, there was no ultimate redoubt.

On its side, Britain also had to act if it was to challenge the French forces in that area. In 1749, Halifax was founded to act as a naval base, and rapidly grew to be a sizable town and the capital of Nova Scotia. During the 1750s (as indeed in later periods of its history), Halifax was the assembly point for large combined operations of sea and land forces. There were always several ships-of-the-line in its harbor or in the area, and two or three infantry regiments in garrison besides auxiliary troops.

As the eastern part of Nova Scotia developed, its western part increasingly worried the British authorities. It was settled with some 9,000 Acadians of French origin. While there were raids by French and Indians, the great majority of Acadians remained neutral, but to no avail. In the name of "security" Governor Charles Lawrence, who was later to be one of Amherst's brigadiers at Louisbourg, decreed the deportation of the whole populace in July 1755. In what would now be called "ethnic cleansing" thousands were gathered by troops as their farms were torched during August and September. After being concentrated in camps for a time, they were embarked on rickety vessels and dropped off all along the American coast. Family members were often separated, never to see each other again. Hundreds died of sickness and, many say, of grief. This awful deed, which inspired Longfellow's famous poem

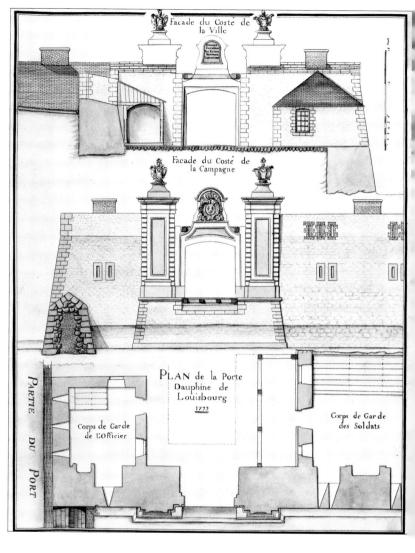

The Dauphin Gate 1733, the main gate leading into Louisbourg. It was next to the Dauphin Bastion. From top to bottom: the gate seen from inside the city, seen from outside, floor plan of the officers' guard house (left) and the soldiers' guard house (right). (National Archives of Canada, C15668)

Evangeline, solved nothing insofar as security was concerned. On the contrary, the situation worsened.

Some Acadians managed to escape and bitterly sought vengeance. They had nothing to lose, with their livelihoods gone and many of their loved ones dead of exposure. Raids on British outposts multiplied. For the British, a simple stroll on the outskirts of Halifax was no longer a safe endeavor. In June 1755, the French frontier forts of Beauséjour and Gaspareau at the straits of Chignectou were captured by British and New England troops which secured the frontier leading to the western part of Nova Scotia. However, following the deportation of the Acadians, the situation became so unsafe that entire regiments had to be posted to that area. The soldiers hardly dared leave their forts, and even wood-cutting parties required heavy escorts as John Knox's journal (published in 1769) tells us. Some of the Acadians had become experts at partisan warfare and were assisted by Abenakis and Micmac Indians. Arms and supplies were sent while, from Canada, officers well versed in bush warfare arrived to train these bitter men. The most notable was Lt. Charles de Boishébert.

All this had immediate repercussions in the whole area. If the Acadian raiders could maintain a permanent threat on the frontier and if a sufficient French naval force could be kept in Louisbourg to threaten the western coast of Nova Scotia, the British colony would be hemmed in, just like the western frontiers of Massachusetts and other New England colonies had been for half a century by the French and Indians.

The attack on Louisbourg in 1745. The Royal Navy's contribution is enhanced in this English print.

OPPOSING PLANS

BRITISH PLANS

The local Acadian grievances coincided with the outbreak of the Seven Years War in Europe (1756–63). If Britain and New England were to break this French-backed stranglehold, vast military and naval resources would be required. Lord Loudoun, commander-in-chief in North America during 1756–57, had devised the master strategy for the conquest of New France. It called for three powerful armies to attack, through the Ohio Valley, by Lake Champlain and by the St Lawrence River. The ultimate objective was for all three armies to meet at Montreal. Great resources would be needed for such a plan to succeed, but approval was obtained from Prime Minister William Pitt and the highest political authorities in Britain. This shifted the main emphasis of the British war effort to America.

British troops were sent to New England in unprecedented numbers, while the various American colonies raised more "provincial" regiments than ever before. Loudoun's strategic plan also required a near-perfect control of the seas, especially the North Atlantic, by the Royal Navy. At the beginning of the Seven Years War the French fleet was certainly the weaker contender after decades of neglect by its government; however, it was still the second most powerful navy in the world and it would take three years for the British to subdue it. This was especially vital for that part of the British plan which called for the invasion of Canada via the St Lawrence and up to Quebec. Such a project was unthinkable without first taking Fortress Louisbourg, France's most powerful naval base in North America. It was impossible to by-pass Louisbourg and leave such a dangerous haven for a French squadron. So, Louisbourg simply had to be taken and that could only be done once naval opposition had been neutralized.

Once that was done, the problem would be to land. This was crucial to the success of the whole campaign. The shores around Louisbourg are very rocky and the only real beach nearby is at La Cormorandière (also called Kennington Cove). This is where the New Englanders had landed in 1745, and Boscawen and Amherst decided to try it again in 1758. Once landed and entrenched safely in a fortified camp, the British

William Pitt the Elder (1708–78), the architect of Britain's overseas imperial and maritime strategy, which resulted in the fall of New France and of French India. Created Earl of Chatham in 1766, he is shown wearing his peer's robe. (Print after R. Brompton)

John Campbell, Earl of Loudoun, conceived the strategic masterplan for the British conquest of New France. It called for the capture of Louisbourg in 1757, but the French navy's ability to assemble a large fleet in the port foiled British ambitions and cost Loudoun his command. In this print, after Allan Ramsay's portrait, Loudoun wears the uniform of his Highland regiment disbanded in 1748. The officers of Fraser's 78th Highlanders at Louisbourg probably wore similar uniforms, as one of them mentioned they wore Loudoun's "livery" of scarlet faced white with gold lace.

would try to take control of the Royal Battery (called the Grand Battery by the British), which covered the inner harbor; with it, they could then shoot at the French warships within. Another important target was Lighthouse Point as it commanded the Island Battery at the harbor's entrance; a strong battery artillery emplacement might reduce the French battery on the island. The rest of the siege operations would be the classic encirclement tactics. The various heights would be captured and the British would close in, building batteries and trenches, until they reached to the town's walls. Eventually, the bombardments would become very intense, a breach would be made and a general assault would be launched.

FRENCH PLANS

France's main emphasis for the war was not in America but in Germany, where most of its army was deployed, notably in the invasion of Hanover, then one of the realms of King George II of Great Britain. Grand strategists in Versailles were not much concerned with naval matters. In spite of this attitude, senior officials of the French navy did all they could to deploy their

squadrons in the North Atlantic, and were reasonably successful in 1756 and 1757.

Officers in Louisbourg did not expect that the navy could protect them forever and made various repairs and improvements to the fortifications. Ideally, the British would not be able to secure a beachhead, but the French were under no great illusions, as there were several places they could land. They built remarkably good field fortifications that covered the length of Cormorandière Cove, consisting of *abbatis* on the beach, backed up by trenches with swivel guns and 6-pdr. guns. Should the British succeed in landing and investing the town, the French could only hope to destroy and deny them everything which might be useful to the besiegers for a long as possible. Lighthouse Point was indefensible and would have to be abandoned. The French ships in the harbor would be outclassed against the British armada outside, but could be very useful as floating batteries to hinder field works as long as possible. It was also hoped that a strong party of Canadians, Acadians and Indians would harass the outer perimeter of the British troops. By all these means, it was hoped to delay the capture of the town for as long as possible.

RIGHT **Model of Louisbourg in c.1750–58 as seen from the east. At the middle right, the wooden barracks built by the British and New Englanders in the Queen's Bastion. Below it was the Princess Bastion (partly visible) which was connected to the Brouillant Bastion via a long wall; on the other side of the gate is the larger Maurepas Bastion with 14 guns of 8 and 24 caliber. The town's main battery was the Pièce de la Grave wall covering the inner harbor with 27 large cannons of 24 and 36 caliber. (Fortress Louisbourg National Historic Site, Louisbourg, Nova Scotia)**

THE FAILED BRITISH NAVAL CAMPAIGNS OF 1756 AND 1757

LEFT Model of Louisbourg in c.1750–58 as seen from the west. Note the Dauphin Bastion's gun positions as rebuilt by the British are now turned around and somewhat elevated to cover the landward side rather than the harbor. In 1758, it held 15 cannons of 18 and 24 caliber. The "Eperon" in the harbor was mounted with six guns of 24 and 12 caliber. The King's Bastion had 18 guns of 8, 18 and 24 caliber. (Fortress Louisbourg National Historic Site, Louisbourg, Nova Scotia)

It is often believed that the Royal Navy dominated the seas unopposed during the Seven Years War. This was not as clear-cut during the first years of the war. Admiral Boscawen's action against the French fleet carrying troops to Canada and Isle Royale in 1755 had been deceitful to the last degree as France and Britain were still at peace. When the *Lys* and the *Alcide* asked the nearing British warships if war had been declared, they were answered with broadsides. In the event, the rest of the French fleet made it safely to Quebec and Louisbourg. War was formally declared on 18 May 1756.

News of Boscawen's action had, by then, long reached Europe and operations had started in the Mediterranean. French Vice-Admiral La Galissonière heading the Toulon fleet engaged and drove off Vice-Admiral Byng's British fleet on 20 May 1756. This opened the way for Marshal Richelieu's army to land on Minorca. After a series of brilliant moves by the French army and a gallant defense by the British garrison, Port Mahon fell on 29 June. The French now dominated the western Mediterranean with the British holding only Gibraltar. All this

Drummer, colonial *Compagnies franches de la Marine*, c. 1755-60. Drummers wore the royal livery of blue lined with red and garnished with the royal livery lace of red or crimson with a white chain. The plate shows the lace on the breast set in large horizontal "U" shaped loops which were increasingly popular by the mid-18th century. There was a shortage of drummers' uniforms during part of 1756 and 1757, so drummers in Louisbourg wore white soldiers' coats with livery lace set on the sleeves, red waistcoats, blue breeches and stockings. The regular uniforms arrived later in 1757. Reconstruction by Eugène Lelièpvre. (Parks Canada)

eventually resulted in the execution of Admiral Byng, "to encourage" the other British admirals as Voltaire wittily put it, but, for the present, the British mastery of the seas was far from assured.

French Commodore Beaussier de l'Isle left Brest in May 1756 leading a small squadron which brought the Marquis de Montcalm to Canada with two further army battalions to reinforce its garrison. Unhindered, the French squadron then sailed from Quebec to Isle Royale and arrived in the vicinity of Louisbourg during the last week of July. The French warships immediately drove off the small British vessels that had been attempting to blockade Louisbourg harbor.

On 26 July, part of the Royal Navy's squadron from Halifax came into view. It consisted of HMS *Grafton* (70 guns), HMS *Nottingham* (60 guns), and the frigates HMS *Hornet* and HMS *Jamaica* led by Commodore Charles Holmes. Beaussier's ships were *Le Héros*, normally of 74 guns but now of only 46 because of the amount of space having been taken by troops and supplies, *L'Illustre* (64 guns), and the frigates *La Sirène* (36 guns), and *La Licorne* (30 guns). Beaussier was in a fighting mood but he restrained himself and first went into Louisbourg to land the supplies vital for the fortress garrison. The next day, he came out of Louisbourg harbor on board *Le Héros*, reinforced by 200 men in the garrison (it was said that the whole garrison volunteered to join him), and, unsupported by *L'Illustre*, immediately engaged Holmes. A series of "indecisive" actions ensued over the following days, the main results of which seem to have been that the main mast of HMS *Jamaica* was shot off rendering the frigate useless. The French went back to Louisbourg and the British to Halifax to make repairs and land the wounded. Beaussier stayed in Louisbourg until the middle of August until, satisfied that nothing much would be attempted against Louisbourg that year, he finally sailed for France. His unscathed squadron was joined by the frigate *Concorde*, out from Quebec, on the way back. Clearly, in 1756, the French navy prevailed.

British plans for 1757 called for massive resources in troops and ships to be committed to the assault on New France. More Americans would be recruited to push forward in the Ohio Valley and up Lake George to Lake Champlain. More importantly, additional ships were to be sent to Nova Scotia, where many regular regiments, mostly sent from Britain, assembled. Once the French had been swept from the surrounding seas, the British would attack Louisbourg. Such was Lord Loudoun's plan. Vice-Admiral Francis Holburne commanded the fleet that was to carry the British army from Halifax to Louisbourg. To do so, he had been granted some 23 warships by the Admiralty.

The French admiralty had mooted some plans of its own for the 1757 campaign in America. Each of the large naval bases, Toulon, Brest, and Rochefort, were to detach a number of ships to America which would rendezvous at Louisbourg in mid-June. French spies were reporting persistent rumors that something substantial would be tried by the British

18

French ships-of-the-line going into action. French warships were noted for their good design and elaborate decorations. Note the great plain white standard which was then France's naval ensign and was also raised on French forts. Before the French Revolution, this was France's fighting flag and had no associations with surrender. (Print after J. Camoreyt)

against Louisbourg. The presence of a strong squadron, even for a short time, might spoil their plans. Admiral Dubois de la Motte coordinated the effort, which was designed to guarantee Louisbourg's safety "from the plans the enemy has made against it, and for which it appears they wish to secure success by immense preparations, and an expenditure which is almost unbelievable."

For once, the French plans worked quite well and they had their share of luck, something they would not see much of in the future years of the Seven Years War. In January 1757, Commodore De Beauffremont sailed four ships-of-the-line from Brest to the West Indies. He reached Haiti on 19 March and sailed north on 4 May, arriving in Louisbourg on

31 May. In April 1757, four ships-of-the-line sailed from Toulon in the Mediterranean under Commodore Du Revest, foiled the attempt of Admiral Saunder's British squadron to stop them at Gibraltar, and arrived unscathed at Louisbourg on 19 June. Meanwhile, Admiral Dubois de La Motte sailed out of Brest with nine ships-of-the-line and two frigates. On board were two battalions of the Berry Regiment which were being sent to Canada as reinforcements for Montcalm's army. The British blockading vessels had been dispersed by a gale but the French accounts do not mention them and the squadron was not much hindered by the Royal Navy. Thus, Admiral Dubois de La Motte's powerful fleet sailed in and weighed anchor unhindered at Louisbourg harbor on 20 June.

The end result of all these French naval movements, and the apparent Royal Navy powerlessness to do anything about it, was that a most worrisome force of French navy vessels was now assembled in Louisbourg harbor. On 20 June 1757, the list of warships stood as follows:

Rear-Admiral Sir Charles Saunders. His squadron at Gibraltar failed to intercept the French ships going to Louisbourg in 1757. He was nevertheless a fine sailor and commanded the British fleet at Quebec in 1759. Portrait by R. Brompton. (National Archives of Canada, C96624)

Le Formidable 80 guns	Le Tonnant 80 guns
Le Duc de Bourgogne 80 guns	Le Défenseur 74 guns
Le Héros 74 guns	Le Diadème 74 guns
L'Hector 74 guns	Le Glorieux 74 guns
Le Dauphin Royal 70 guns	Le Superbe 70 guns
L'Achilles 64 guns	L'Eveillé 64 guns
Le Vaillant 64 guns	L'Inflexible 64 guns
Le Belliqueux 64 guns	Le Sage 64 guns
Le Bizarre 64 guns	Le Célèbre 64 guns
L'Abénakise 36 guns	La Bonne 32 guns
La Fleur de Lys 32 guns	La Comète 32 guns
L'Herminione 26 guns	

This made a total of 18 ships-of-the-line and five frigates. In July, the frigates cruised to the north and to the south-west of Cape Breton Island but did not find any traces of the British. At the end of July, it was learned from various prisoners taken by French and Indian scouting parties lurking in the vicinity of Halifax that the British fleet had arrived, consisting of 16 ships-of-the-line and six frigates. The informants further stated that some 12 to 15,000 men, "part of which came from Boston," formed the army that was to sail to besiege Louisbourg.

French intelligence of British movements was good and confirmed what had been strongly suspected for sometime: that the British were planning a large expedition to take the fortress. In the spring, Governor Drucour had asked Boishébert, who led the Acadian volunteers on the St John's River, to come closer to Louisbourg with his men. In July, Boishébert arrived on Isle Royale with some 400 Acadians and Indians and positioned themselves in the area of Gabarus Bay, where a landing seemed likely.

Drucour's defense plan called for as much resistance as possible to be waged outside the walls of the city. If the British did come, the garrison would emerge to fight them on the beaches and in the woods, "as it was likely", wrote the Chevalier de Vaudreuil, "that the enemy would loose a lot of men" before approaching "some distance from the city." Admiral Dubois de La Motte detached sailors from his ships to help speed up the repairs to the fortifications and soon, grass was laid on the refurbished King's Bastion. To strengthen the garrison, a battalion of 12 temporary companies, each of 50 ships' marines led by two officers, and a further four companies of ships' volunteers intended to serve the guns, were organized and went into town. The volunteers were made up of petty officers and pilots led by naval officers; all of which added some 800 men to the garrison besides Boishébert's men.

On 7 August, the companies of ships' marines and volunteers were marched out of town with three of the garrisons' companies and posted

Halifax, Nova Scotia, c.1758–59. Founded in 1749 largely to counter the French in Louisbourg, Halifax swiftly became the Royal Navy's main base in the North Atlantic. (National Archives of Canada, C54)

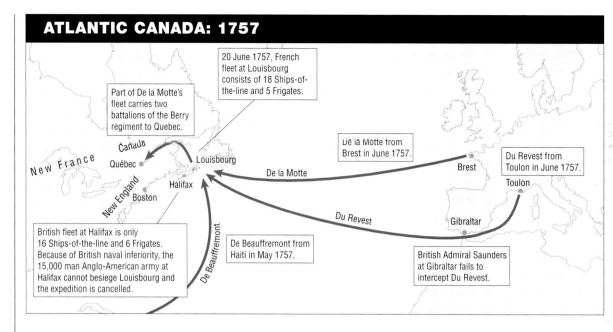

20 June 1757, French fleet at Louisbourg consists of 18 Ships-of-the-line and 5 Frigates.

Part of De la Motte's fleet carries two battalions of the Berry regiment to Quebec.

De la Motte from Brest in June 1757.

Du Revest from Toulon in June 1757.

British fleet at Halifax is only 16 Ships-of-the-line and 6 Frigates. Because of British naval inferiority, the 15,000 man Anglo-American army at Halifax cannot besiege Louisbourg and the expedition is cancelled.

De Beauffremont from Haiti in May 1757.

British Admiral Saunders at Gibraltar fails to intercept Du Revest.

in prepared positions and temporary batteries at three coves to the east of the city. Makeshift tents and awnings for theses troops were made from old sails and everyone settled down to wait for the British.

On the afternoon of 19 August, a British squadron was spotted to the south-east and, the next day, it came in closer, seemingly to see if the French fleet was still in Louisbourg harbor. Vice-Admiral Holburne was hoping to lure Dubois de la Motte's squadron out of the harbor for a general engagement. The planned expedition was by now ruined, but Holburne hoped to damage, if not defeat, the French squadron. Otherwise, the whole season's campaign was wasted and nothing further could be done until the following year. The British squadron was observed by the French to be made up of 16 ships-of-the-line, four frigates and what appeared to be a bomb ketch. Dubois de la Motte, for his part, was a wise old sea dog and not about to be lured into dividing his forces, which would inevitably happen if his ships sailed out one after the other from the narrow harbor entrance. They would be at a numerical disadvantage until they could form a battle line. There was nothing to be gained by going out to attack and plenty to gain by waiting for the British, reasoned Dubois de la Motte. The British no doubt observed that the French fleet and the Louisbourg garrison were ready for a fight should they attack and, after an hour or so, Holburne's ships turned and sailed away. Fog covered the departing British and they were not seen again in the following days. On 27 August, the ship's marines and volunteer temporary companies were dissolved and everyone went back on board as Admiral Dubois de La Motte felt that his ships should be at full strength if there was to be a battle with the British.

Holburne kept his position off Louisbourg. The British squadron, now observed by the French to consist of 23 sails, came back within sight of Louisbourg on 16 September. Again, the British ships came almost to within cannon range of the fortress guns, loitered for a few days in the area and then left. Dubois de La Motte knew there was nothing to gain by chasing them; Louisbourg was safe as long as his squadron was in the harbor. Besides the British fleet, there was much concern in the French camp concerning the British army in Halifax, which was reputed to be very strong. A French scouting party had just returned from Halifax on 21 September. It reported having seen about 1,200 tents with red-coated troops drilling, but there seemed to be many empty tents and it appeared that some of the troops had gone back to New England or Europe. Furthermore, there were very few ships in Halifax harbor. All this seemed to indicate that the attack had been canceled.

Holburne's squadron remained off Louisbourg. On 25 September, gale-force winds sank HMS *Tilbury* (60 guns), and seriously damaged the other British ships, forcing Holburne to cancel any further attempt to intercept the French fleet. Instead, he had to put into Halifax for repairs. The gale, the worst in many years, also damaged the French fleet, but much less seriously as it was relatively sheltered in Louisbourg's harbor. After having the damage repaired on the *Tonnant*, Dubois de la Motte and his squadron sailed out of Louisbourg and returned safely to France.

In England, a distraught William Pitt reflected the mood of the British public. The 1757 campaign in America was a shambles. Nothing much had been done in the Ohio Valley. Montcalm had taken Fort William-Henry in July and the ensuing massacre of prisoners had enraged public opinion further. Now came the cancellation of the attack on Louisbourg which had been prepared at great expense. This was too much to bear; politicians and the public demanded a scapegoat. Thus, the commander-in-chief in North America, Lord Loudoun, the architect of the strategy that would ultimately conquer New France, was recalled to England.

Far from discouraged, the British brought in even greater resources for the campaign of 1758. Although he was replaced by Maj. Gen. James Abercromby, Lord Loudoun's strategic plan was to be implemented even more fully. Gen. Forbes would march into the Ohio Valley, take Fort Duquesne (now Pittsburgh) and finally avenge Gen. Braddock's disastrous defeat at Monongahela three years earlier in July 1755. The commander-in-chief, Gen. Abercromby, would lead the largest Anglo-American army ever assembled in North America, take Fort Carillon at Ticonderoga and secure the Lake Champlain area. Britain's largest commitment in terms of manpower and resources was to be concentrated on the expedition against Fortress Louisbourg to be commanded by a new and relatively young general, Jeffery Amherst.

Battalion color, Isle Royale *Compagnies franches de la Marine*, 1740s and 1750s. In 1758, they had to surrender their colors to the British, who took them, with other colors, to St Paul's, where their silk had totally disintegrated by 1840. Meanwhile, the Isle Royale *Compagnies franches* were repatriated to France and granted new colors in 1759. Following their disbandment in December 1760, the new colors were stored for a few years until sent to the garrison infantry of French Guyana. Reconstruction by Michel Pétard. (Canadian Department of National Defence)

OPPOSING COMMANDERS

THE BRITISH

Jeffery Amherst (1717–97) was born in Riverhead, Kent, into a family of successful lawyers – both his father and his grandfather had been called to the bar. The choice of military careers for three of the Amherst sons was influenced by a close friend of the family, Lionel Sackville, Duke of Dorset. In 1735, Jeffery was commissioned as an ensign in the 1st Foot Guards. In 1741, the regiment went to Flanders and the following year, Maj. Gen. John Ligonier noticed young Amherst and appointed him as his aide-de-camp. The new ADC was exposed to general staff duties, work for which his methodical character was ideally suited. His first battle was Dettingen in 1743, followed by Marshal Saxe's victory at Fontenoy in 1745. Recalled to Britain because of the Jacobite uprising, he was back in Flanders the following year. In 1747, no doubt on Ligonier's recommendation, Amherst became ADC to the Duke of Cumberland, King George II's son and commander-in-chief of the British contingent on the Continent. Amherst campaigned with the duke until the end of hostilities in 1748. Following the war, Amherst remained attached to the duke's personal staff as well as being a guards officer. He was now in good standing with the highest circles at court.

With the outbreak of war in 1756, he was sent to Germany to perform staff work and, the following year, was again under the Duke of Cumberland. He also obtained the colonelcy of the 15th Foot. The duke was, however, totally out-maneuvered by the French army and had to sign the Kloster Zeven Convention, which practically signed away Hanover. A furious George II recalled his disgraced son and repudiated the convention. Ligonier was appointed commander-in-chief of the British army. In January 1758, Amherst was recalled to England. William Pitt had heard of the competent and experienced colonel and presented Amherst with the great opportunity of his life: to command the army that would attack Louisbourg with the rank of major-general in America. Although no doubt influenced by Ligonier's recommendations and Amherst's own fine soldierly qualities, the appointment was a remarkable act of faith on Pitt's part. Amherst had

Vice-Admiral Edward Hawke was nowhere near Louisbourg in 1758, but his contribution was nevertheless important, as in March he prevented the departure for America of a French squadron. He went on to become Admiral of the Fleet and is shown here in the dress uniform worn from 1767. (Print after Francis Cotes)

Sir John Ligonier, commander-in-chief of the British army in 1758, secured the services of Jeffery Amherst as commander of the Louisbourg expedition.

never held any previous field commands and was inexperienced in the coordination of military and naval forces. As it turned out, the stolid and unemotional Amherst was an excellent choice. He was a methodical soldier, shrewdly calculating the elements in his favor without ever losing sight of the ultimate goal which must be victory.

His conduct at Louisbourg fully revealed his capacity as an effective senior commander. He quickly saw that his keenest and best brigadier was young James Wolfe and used him to the fullest. In spite of his dour personality, it was Amherst's ability to communicate efficiently, delegate powers with discernment and maintain good relations on the staff that made him commander-in-chief in North America in 1759. That year, he carried Ticonderoga and, in September 1760, received the surrender of the French forces in Canada at Montreal. He had, by then, coordinated the approach of three British armies to meet in Montreal, thus achieving the final objective of Lord Loudoun's strategic plan. After the war, he went on to become commander-in-chief of the British army and was elevated to the peerage. As a last honor, he was made field marshal in 1795. Jeffery Amherst's personal character is perhaps best defined by Sir Nathaniel William Wraxall, MP, who knew him well and wrote that "his manners were grave, formal and cold," that he was "naturally taciturn and reserved," and that "he usually gave his decided affirmative or negative ... in a few words." As a whole, he was seen by Wraxall as "disinterested, of an elevated mind, that aspired beyond the accumulation of money. His judgement was sound and his understanding solid, but neither cultivated by education or expanded by elegant knowledge."

James Wolfe (1727–59) obtained his commission in 1741 and went to Flanders, his first battle being Dettingen, like Amherst. He then served against the Jacobites in Scotland. After the '45 he went back to Flanders and was wounded at Laffeldt on 2 July 1747 where the Anglo-Dutch

Sir Jeffery Amherst, officer commanding the British land forces at the 1758 siege of Louisbourg. (Print after Sir Joshua Reynolds)

Maj. Gen. James Wolfe, in the full-red uniform that he usually wore during the siege of Quebec and probably during the siege of Louisbourg also. This uniform dated from the days of Marlborough as an optional field dress for officers. (Print by J. S. C. Schaak, after a sketch by Hervey Smith)

forces were defeated by Marshal de Saxe. He spent the years of peace from 1748 with his unit, traveling to Ireland and Paris, and studying Latin and mathematics. War was declared in 1756 and, the following year, Wolfe was selected as quartermaster-general of the forces for the abortive raid on Rochefort. In spite of the raid's failure, Wolfe's reputation emerged intact, as he had advised a less cautious approach to the operation, and he was promoted to colonel. Recognized as a bright and professional officer, Wolfe arrived in Halifax in early May 1758 to serve as brigadier under Jeffery Amherst in the expedition against Louisbourg. His dash ashore with his men in spite of many obstacles carried the day, and his later actions during the siege were excellent. His gallantry at Louisbourg gave him credibility as a promising commander and, back in England at the end of 1758, he made the most of it by obtaining the command of the expedition against Quebec in 1759 (see the work by the same author *Order of Battle 3: Quebec 1759*, Oxford, Osprey, 1999).

Charles Lawrence (1709–60) went into the army in 1727 and served in North America in 1729 and in the West Indies from 1733 to 1737. Back in Europe, he fought in Flanders during the War of the Austrian Succession, being wounded at Fontenoy in 1745. He first went to Louisbourg as part of its British garrison in 1747 and moved on to Nova Scotia in 1748. In 1753, he became lieutenant-governor of Nova Scotia and, in 1755, was largely responsible for the deportation of the Acadians before moving on to the military duties that were obviously more suited to his somewhat stern personality. His knowledge of Nova Scotia and of the army made him a good choice to act as brigadier.

Edward Whitmore (1691–1761) was colonel of the 22nd Foot from 1757. A soldier of long-standing experience, he was chosen as a brigadier for the Louisbourg expedition but does not always seem to have carried out his duties with all the energy that Amherst would have wished. This is not too surprising as Whitmore was then 65 years old. His wisdom must nevertheless have been appreciated for, after the town's surrender, he was made its governor.

John Henry Bastide (*c.* 1700–70) was the chief engineer of the expedition with the rank of colonel. He was an able professional with a long experience of North America. His personal interest in Louisbourg went back to the 1730s and, in 1745, he helped in the preparation of the New Englander's campaign. After serving at Minorca, he returned to America to undertake the intricate conventional siege operations that would be required at Louisbourg. He had a staff of ten engineers to assist him during the campaign, which they did most competently, especially as Bastide was incapacitated for part of the siege.

Vice-Admiral Edward Boscawen, commander-in-chief of the British fleet at Louisbourg in 1758. He raised his flag on the 90-gun HMS *Namur*. (Print after Sir Joshua Reynolds)

The Honourable Edward Boscawen (1711–61) was the son of Viscount Falmouth and a largely absentee Member of Parliament for many years. He entered the Royal Navy in 1726, and obtained his first command in 1737. He distinguished himself in command of HMS *Shoreham* at Porto Bello (Panama) and in the failed Cartagena de Indias (Colombia) expedition in 1741. He attained flag rank in 1747 and was wounded at Cape Finistère but went on to the East Indies. Although the British forces failed to take Pondicherry in 1748, Boscawen gained experience that would later prove useful in Louisbourg. Back in England in 1750, he was made vice-admiral and spent the next years as a member of the Admiralty Board. With a reputation as a bluff sailor, he was sometimes nicknamed "Wry-neck Dick" and "Old Dreadnought," which gives an idea of his character. An aggressively skilled tactician, he spent much of 1755 at sea trying to intercept the French fleet bringing troops to Canada. In 1756, he was the senior naval commander at Portsmouth and, a year later, served with Sir Edward Hawke at the naval blockade of Brest which was not without its flaws as French warships got in and out.

The assault on Louisbourg was a major expedition which required an experienced fleet commander, and Pitt appointed Boscawen to command the fleet, which arrived in Halifax on 9 May 1758. Boscawen's direction of the fleet at the siege of Louisbourg was notable for the excellent coordination with the land forces, as can be seen by Amherst's journal of the siege operations. Boscawen took an active role in the military operations, assisting brigadiers Lawrence and Wolfe in the first draft of the assault plan and providing landing craft training to the troops. He sent guns and sailors with skills in gunnery, mining, woodwork, etc., ashore to help the siege operations. Amherst was fortunate to have the support of such a fine naval commander. Following the capture of Louisbourg, Boscawen went back to Europe to command the Western Squadron and, in 1759, shattered a French fleet off Lagos, Portugal. However, almost worn out, he fell ill in December 1760 and died in January 1761.

Sir Charles Hardy (1716–80) entered the Royal Navy in 1731, and became a captain ten years later. After a short tenure as governor of New York in 1755, Sir Charles rose to flag rank in 1756 and was second-in-command to Holburne during the failed Louisbourg operations of 1757. This fine sailor and able tactician was a good second-in-command to Admiral Boscawen, as he was familiar with the peculiar sea conditions around Cape Breton Island. Following the siege, he returned to Europe and was again second-in-command at Admiral Hawke's brilliant victory at Quiberon in 1759, a decisive action which crippled the French Atlantic fleet.

THE FRENCH

Chevalier Augustin de Boschenry de Drucour (1703–62), governor of Isle Royale and officer commanding the French during the siege, was born in Normandy and entered the navy in 1719. Over the next 30 years, he participated in some 16 naval campaigns which took him to Sweden, Turkey, the West Indies and North America. He was captured by the British on board the *Mars* in 1746, but was released the following year. He was made a knight of the Order of Saint-Louis in 1749 and promoted to ship-of-the-line captain in 1751. A competent and brave officer with much experience at sea, he became the commandant in Brest of the select naval cadet unit, the *Gardes du Pavillion Amiral* (Guards of the Admiral's Flag). In 1754, Drucour was selected to be the governor of Isle Royale and he arrived with his wife at Louisbourg in mid-August.

As the ministry of the navy was responsible for the administration of France's American colonies, the colonial governors were nearly always experienced naval officers. Drucour had many difficulties regarding lack of money and supplies during his tenure but, working with Commissaire-Ordonnateur Jacques Prévost de La Croix, the colony's chief administrative officer, the magazines were kept reasonably full. As a commander, he saw that the troops were well disciplined and in good spirits in spite of Louisbourg's isolation – not an easy task on Isle Royale. Although he received some reinforcements during the war, he knew his position was practically hopeless unless the French navy could provide a strong enough squadron. This was impossible in 1758 in the face of Admiral Boscawen's formidable fleet and, in his soul, Drucour had

Private, Bourgogne Infantry Regiment, *c.* 1757. (Musée de l'Armée, Paris)

slim hopes of gaining the advantages against such superior forces. He nevertheless proved a very spirited commander and gave considerable resistance to the British with the resources at hand. Although mortified at not being granted the "honors of war" when the French surrendered, he bowed to Amherst's harsh terms to protect the civilians from further harm. However, his brave stand earned him the respect of the British commanders who treated him with "every honor due to his rank." Drucour, a man of great integrity, was totally ruined by his tenure as governor. Back in France, he had to live on the charity of his brother until he and his wife obtained pensions. His health had also been impaired, and he died at Le Havre in August 1762.

Henri-Mathieu Marchant de la Houlière (1717–93), commandant-general of the French garrison, was an experienced army officer who had participated in nine sieges in Europe. He was therefore a good choice to be commandant-general of the troops in Louisbourg in the event of a British attack. The setback for the French was that he was appointed much too late; he arrived on 31 May and took up his duties the next day, 1 June. A day later, the British fleet was in sight nearing Louisbourg. With hardly any time to become familiar with the fortress, its immediate area and its garrison, de la Houlière nevertheless performed quite well during the siege. During the landing on 8 June, it was noted that "M. de la Houlière, commandant general of our troops was nearly hit by a cannon ball," (WO 34/101) but he escaped injury during the rest of the siege.

Jean-Antoine Charry, Marquis Desgouttes entered the navy in 1725 as a *Garde de la Marine* (naval cadet) and achieved the rank of captain of a ship-of-the-line in 1746. Captain of *L'Entreprenant* trapped in Louisbourg during the siege, he was the senior naval officer present and did all he could to be a nuisance to the British. Fighting against overwhelming odds, his squadron's resistance in the harbor only ended when the ships were finally destroyed, which, coupled with the breaches in the walls, finally provoked the surrender. Desgouttes' stubborn fight was acknowledged in France and he retired with the pension of a vice-admiral in 1764.

Louis-Joseph Beaussier de L'Isle (1701–65) entered the French navy in 1724, served with distinction in Europe and was made ship-of-the-line captain in 1749 and Chevalier de Saint-Louis the following year. In 1756, Beaussier commanded the squadron bringing Gen. Montcalm to Quebec, then headed for Louisbourg. In late July he compelled Royal Navy Commodore Holmes to withdraw from the vicinity of Louisbourg, adding to his reputation as a "fighting captain" as well as a skilled sailor. After a period of illness, he returned to Louisbourg with a small squadron in 1758 and served under Commodore Desgouttes, who was the senior naval officer in port. Beaussier was really at his best under sail in the open seas, and although his naval talents were unusable shut in port, he ably did what he could in the defense. He was later promoted to head a fleet to raid the Portuguese in Brazil but the expedition was canceled with the end of hostilities in 1763.

Louis Franquet (1697–1768), a colonel of engineers, was an experienced officer who had served in many campaigns and sieges in Europe. In 1754, Franquet supervised the restoration of Louisbourg's defenses, assisted by Claude-Victor Grillot de Poilly, Michel de Couagne and two other officers. Franquet saw no virtue in the Royal Battery, and demolished it, which saved the French warships in the harbor from being destroyed by the British. During the siege, Franquet was very ill, so it was left to Grillot and his engineers to repair and adapt the bombarded works under impossible odds.

French naval Commodore Louis-Joseph Beaussier de l'Isle (1701–65), whose squadron, in 1756, kept the Royal Navy at bay in a series of naval engagements off Louisbourg. He was back in Louisbourg in 1758 but was trapped by Boscawen's fleet. He and his men helped Drucour put up a stubborn resistance during the siege. (National Archives of Canada, C44821)

OPPOSING ARMIES

THE BRITISH

The bulwark of the British army sent out to take Louisbourg was the contingent of some 14 battalions draw from 13 line infantry regiments. Unlike the two other British armies in North America which had many colonial American provincial troops, Amherst's army only had 500 American rangers in addition to the 12,300 officers and enlisted men from regular units.

In terms of seniority, the 1st Foot was the oldest regiment, and wags called it "Pontius Pilate's Bodyguard" because of its claims to ancient lineage. Other units had been raised in Britain and Ireland in the late-17th and early-18th centuries except for the 58th, the 60th, and the 78th. The 58th was raised in Britain from 1755 and was sent to North America in 1757. The 60th was a multi-battalion unit intended to be raised in America from 1755, but plans were revised and the "Royal Americans" were largely recruited from Germans and Swiss. The

Battalion color, 1st Foot (Royal Scots), 1750s. The second battalion was present at Louisbourg.

Two officers of the 78th Foot (Fraser's Highlanders), 1759–60. This detail from a print, after Richard Short, is possibly the only period representation of this unit. (National Archives of Canada, C361)

78th, raised in the Scottish Highlands in 1757, was originally numbered the 63rd and many documents on the siege still gave it that number, although it was renumbered 78th on 21 April 1757. Except for the 1st and the 60th, the regiments only had one battalion, which was the usual practice in the British infantry. Each battalion was divided into ten companies including one of grenadiers, the elite soldiers who wore pointed miter caps (the "hat men" in the other so-called "battalion companies" wore tricorns). They were armed with the dependable "Brown Bess" Long Land-pattern musket with bayonet and hanger. Their red uniforms had various distinctive regimental facings and lace, and were, in general, the same as those of British soldiers in Europe. The 78th was the exception. Its men, many of whom only spoke Gaelic, wore short red jackets and belted plaid kilts instead of breeches and gaiters. Highlanders also formed the strongest of the units in Amherst's army. They carried a slightly shorter musket with bayonet, and were armed in Highland fashion with broadsword, pistols, and dirks.

Three companies of the Royal Artillery totaling 267 gunners and bombardiers were attached to the expedition to serve the train of artillery. They were often assisted by sailors familiar with artillery, and by some 200 miners, again recruited from the fleet's sailors. In all, there

FAR LEFT **Officer, Royal Artillery, campaign dress, late 1750s–early-1760s. (Print after R. J. Macdonald based on contemporary portraits)**

LEFT **Private, 60th Foot (Royal Americans), 1755–67. The enlisted men's uniform did not have regimental lace. (Print after a reconstruction by P. W. Reynolds)**

OPPOSITE PAGE LEFT **Officer, colonial *Compagnies franches de la Marine*, c. 1750–60. This man is a senior officer as he wears the coveted cross of the Order of Saint-Louis on a scarlet ribbon which also gave the title of "chevalier", the equivalent of the British knight. Gold lace was forbidden on the coat, but was often seen on the waistcoats of the more stylish officers. Reconstruction by Eugène Lelièpvre. (Parks Canada)**

OPPOSITE PAGE CENTER **Private, colonial *Compagnies franches de la Marine*, 1757–58. As shown on this plate, the colonial troops in Louisbourg were issued in 1757 with the army's 30-round cartridge box suspended by its own buff belt. Reconstruction by Eugène Lelièpvre. (Parks Canada)**

OPPOSITE PAGE RIGHT **Gunner, *Canonniers-Bombardiers*, c. 1755–60. The colonial artillery had blue uniforms faced with red like the metropolitan artillery, but wore white metal hat lace and buttons rather than the yellow metal worn by Royal-Artillerie. When not attending the guns, the colonial gunners acted as grenadiers and carried muskets, bayonets and sabers as shown. Reconstruction by Eugène Lelièpvre. (Parks Canada)**

were about 1,300 sailors serving on shore. Admiral Boscawen also detached about 500 marines on shore.

Amherst wanted a light infantry corps to oppose the Canadians, Acadians and Indians that would invariably harass the army on Cape Breton Island during the siege. Four companies of New England rangers totaling 500 men were attached to the expedition. They were the companies of captains Benonie Danks, Joseph Gorham, James Rogers and John Stark. Amherst, however, was never impressed by the free-wheeling ways of American rangers and wanted a better-disciplined and more dependable force of British troops to act as light infantry.

On 12 May 1758, he gave orders to form a Provisional Light Infantry Battalion drawn from officers and men in the regular regiments that were best suited for this type of duty. It was commanded by Maj. George Scott, 40th Foot, a man who was familiar with light infantry tactics and bush warfare. Each regiment provided, for the duration of the campaign, 20 to 30 men under a lieutenant, except for the 78th, which detached 100 men. In all, it consisted of "550 Volunteers chosen as Marksmen out of the most active resolute Men" that were "dressed some in blue, some in green Jackets and Drawers, for easier brushing through the Woods; with Ruffs of black Bear's Skin round their Necks, the beard of the upper Lips, some grown into Whiskers, others not so but all well smutted on that part, with little round Hats like several of our Seamen."

Amherst also appointed Scott to have overall command of the American ranger companies as well as over his own light infantry battalion.

THE FRENCH

At Isle Royale, the "*Compagnies franches de la Marine*" (Independent Companies of the Navy) were the regular garrison of colonial infantry. They were named "*Compagnies franches*" because they were organized not into regiments, but as independent companies, and "*de la Marine*" because they were under the jurisdiction of the Ministry of the Navy, rather than the Ministry of War. They were occasionally termed the "*troupes de la colonie*" (the colony's troops). The original establishment of Isle Royale Compagnies franches had been formed in 1713–14 from the Acadia and Placentia garrison companies. Following the first retrocession of Louisbourg to France in 1748, the establishment was tripled from eight to 24 companies by order of 28 March 1749, each company having four officers and 50 enlisted men for a theoretical total of 96 officers and 1,200 men.

Unlike some of the *Compagnies franches* personnel in Canada and Louisiana who were versed in woodcraft and bush warfare, those in Isle Royale were fortress garrison troops in the European style. Some of the officers originated from Louisbourg, but very few enlisted men appear to have settled there, nor were they especially encouraged to do so. After their six years or so of service, they went back to France. Louisbourg was

a naval base and a trading town, not really a settlement colony. Nearly all the companies served in Louisbourg but not all. A company was detached to garrison Port la Joye on Isle Saint-Jean (now Charlottetown on Prince Edward Island). Before the siege, there were also two companies serving at Port Toulouse and one at Port Dauphin. After the siege, the colonial infantrymen were eventually repatriated to Rochefort in France and presented with new colors to replace the ones they had surrendered at Louisbourg. In 1760, some 400 of these Isle Royale soldiers were formed in eight companies and they took part in the ill-fated expedition to Canada which ended in the Restigouche River in July. The remnants of the Isle Royale companies were seemingly incorporated into the metropolitan battalions on 25 December 1760.

Louisbourg had the first regular overseas artillery company formed by royal order of the French colonial army. The *Canonniers-Bombardiers* were formed at Louisbourg following an order of 20 June 1743. The new gunners were chosen from the enlisted men in the colonial infantry that showed the most skill as gunners. A second company was added from 1 February 1758. It was formed at the fortress in the late spring, with a reinforcement of ten gunners from the Rochefort company of the *Bombardiers de la Marine* (one of the French navy's marine artillery

RIGHT **Private, metropolitan** *Compagnies franches de la Marine, c.*1755–60. **This copy of a period manuscript which is now lost, shows the gray-white and blue uniform common to both the colonial and the metropolitan** *Compagnies franches.* **It also shows interesting differences, such as the blue collar and the white anchors on the turnbacks of the metropolitan** *Compagnies franches* **which are also seen on Vernet's renderings. The colonial** *Compagnies franches* **did not have collars and there is no information as to turnback ornaments. (Private collection)**

LEFT **Fusilier,** *Volontaires-Étrangers* **Regiment, 1758. Being a foreign unit, green was used as a facing color on the white uniform rather than red, white or blue which were used by regiments manned by French nationals. The men's usual language was German. Note the Dauphin Gate in the background. Reconstruction by Eugène Lelièpvre. (Canadian Department of National Defence)**

companies) detached to instruct the new gunners. Each company had an establishment of three officers and 50 gunners and bombardiers. These two companies gave exceptional and even heroic services during the siege operations, but the work of these superlative gunners was hardly recognized by the French authorities of the time and has been largely ignored by French military historians since. The remnants of these excellent and brave companies were sent to fever-ridden Haiti in 1762.

The colonial troops in Louisbourg were reinforced by several metropolitan *Troupes de Terre* (land army) battalions. In May 1755, the second battalions of the Bourgogne and Artois regiments arrived under the command of lieutenant-colonels Marin and Saint-Julien respectively. Each battalion had 13 companies, including one of grenadiers mustering 31 officers and 525 enlisted men. The commanders of these two battalions were initially reluctant to defer to a colonial governor as their field officer but they soon acknowledged Chevalier de Drucour's authority and gave very good service.

In 1758, two additional metropolitan battalions were rushed over to Louisbourg. The first to arrive on 28 March was the second battalion of the *Volontaires-Étrangers* Regiment under Lt. Col. d'Anthonay, a foreign unit recruited mostly from Germans. It had 13 companies, including one of grenadiers, and an establishment of 41 officers and 660 enlisted men. Although it gave good service, there were frequent deserters to the British during the siege and it seems that some joined the British after the surrender. The last unit to make it into Louisbourg, just in the nick of time, was the second battalion of the Cambis Regiment under Lt. Col. the Chevalier de Langevin. Its 17 companies (including one of grenadiers) landed at Port Dauphin in early June and marched overland to the fortress, as the Royal Navy was already blockading Louisbourg's harbor. Its establishment of 17 companies reflected the augmentations made in the French infantry: it had an establishment of 40 officers and 685 enlisted men. A sergeant and 26 sick soldiers remained on board Duchassault's squadron and went on to Quebec. Cambis probably had the finest esprit-de-corps of the infantry in the garrison and almost mutinied when they heard they had to surrender.

At the beginning of the siege, Drucour formed five temporary companies or *picquets* of 50 volunteers from each regiment into a light infantry corps. Their first task was to act as scouts and to prevent British raiders from coming too close. Later on, they were posted within cannon range of the city "and sometimes beyond" to raid the enemy in "*petite guerre*" (guerrilla) tactics (WO 34/101).

The garrison also had about 150 marines ("three piquets") from the metropolitan *Compagnies franches de la Marine*, who were distinct from the colonial *Compagnies franches*. Although they wore the same uniforms, they had their own distinct establishment of 100 companies based in France and were the marines that served as infantry on board French warships. Three piquets were detached on land from ships in the harbor, but others served on board their warships during the siege until early July, when most others were landed to serve with the garrison.

Louisbourg was also defended by a Bourgeois Militia amounting to some 300 men, all ranks. About 100 Acadians from Isle Saint-Jean under the command of Villejoin the Younger arrived in Louisbourg just before the siege and were posted at the end of Gabarus Bay; they later joined Boishébert's party.

Acadian partisan, c. 1755–60. Reconstruction by Derek FitzJames. (Fort Beauséjour National Historic Site, Aulac, New Brunswick)

The quality and morale of the troops was quite good and none of the French-born soldiers deserted to the British according to Drucour. However, a few of the German soldiers in the *Volontaires-Étrangers* battalion did, which was to be expected in foreign troops as they always included some "professional deserters" in their ranks. Drucour mentioned that a sortie was canceled because a soldier of *Volontaires-Étrangers* had deserted two hours before the intended sally. Apart from this, the *Volontaires-Étrangers* gave a good account of themselves.

Although not part of the garrison, Boishébert's force played a part, albeit not decisive, in harassing the outside perimeter of the British army. Its nucleus had been formed at Quebec, in the spring of 1758, and consisted, besides Boishébert, of five Canadian colonial troop officers experienced in bush warfare, five Canadian colonial troop cadets and 70 Canadian volunteers some of whom were colonial regular soldiers. They landed from their schooners at Miramichi on 9 June after a rough trip on stormy seas but had few supplies. They were eventually joined by 170 Acadians and 60 Indians, reaching the vicinity of Louisbourg in early July. They skirmished with Amherst's over-whelming force, but sickness set in and up to 60 men were eventually afflicted with anthrax. This frightened the Indians and all deserted. Nevertheless, Boishébert remained in the area until after Louisbourg's surrender. On the way back to Miramichi, he ambushed a strong British detachment at Peticodiac. Boishébert's party was now almost starving with many sick. The party was basically dissolved from mid-August, the officers, the Canadians and many Acadians eventually returning to Canada.

BRITISH ORDER OF BATTLE LOUISBOURG 1758

Maj. Gen. Jeffery Amherst, Officer Commanding

Divisional commanders
Brig. Gen. Edward Whitmore
Brig. Gen. James Wolfe
Brig. Gen. Charles Lawrence

Engineers on the expedition:
Col. John Henry Bastide, Director
Maj. Patrick MacKellar, Sub Director
Capt. Matthew Dixon, Ordinary
Capt. George Weston, Ordinary
Capt. John Brewse, Ordinary
Capt. Lt Hugh Debbing, Extraordinary
Capt. Lt William Bontaine, Extraordinary
Capt. Lt Adam Williamson, Extraordinary
Ens. Augustus Durnford, Practitioner
Ens. William Spry, Practitioner
Ens. John Montresor, Practitioner

Commanding the artillery
Lt. Col. George Williamson

Infantry Regiments
2nd Bn. 1st Foot, (Royal Scots) 44 officers, 910 enlisted men: 954.
15th Foot (Amherst's) 40 officers, 817 enlisted men: 957.
17th Foot (Forbes') 32 officers, 709 enlisted men: 741.
22nd Foot (Whitmore's) 40 officers, 967 enlisted men: 1,007.
28th Foot (Bragg's) 31 officers, 677 enlisted men: 708.
35th Foot (Otway's) 27 officers, 600 enlisted men: 627.
40th Foot (Hopson's) 35 officers, 596 enlisted men: 629.
45th Foot (Warburton's) 35 officers, 921 enlisted men: 956.
47th Foot (Lascelles') 36 officers, 913 enlisted men: 949.
48th Foot (Webb's) 39 offers, 990 enlisted men: 1,029.
58th Foot (Anstruther's) 29 officers, 656 enlisted men: 685.
2nd Bn. 60th Foot (Lawrence's) 29 officers, 984 enlisted men: 1,013.
3rd Bn. 60th Foot (Monckton's) 35 officers, 866 enlisted men: 901.
78th Foot (Fraser's Highlanders) 50 officers, 1,149 enlisted
    men: 1,199.

Total for regiments, 514 officers, 11,787 enlisted men: 12,301.
To which should be added about 15 field and staff officers, four
companies totaling 500 Rangers, 267 Royal Artillery and about
500 Marines and 1,300 sailors serving on shore.
Grand Total: 14,883 land forces.

RIGHT **Private, Royal Artillery,
1750s. Reconstruction by Derek
FitzJames. (Fort Beauséjour
National Historic Site, Aulac,
New Brunswick)**

FAR RIGHT **Private, Warburton's
45th Foot, 1750s. He wears the
brown "marching gaiters" used
in campaign. Reconstruction
by Derek FitzJames. (Fort
Beauséjour National Historic
Site, Aulac, New Brunswick)**

Provisional Light Infantry Battalion

Maj. George Scott

550 men drawn from the regular regiments listed above.

NB: The officers of Rangers, Royal Artillery, and Marines may not be included in the above figures. This would make about 50 officers.

British Ordnance brought in for the siege:

- 2 13-in. brass mortars
- 2 10-in. brass mortars
- 7 8-in. brass mortars
- 10 5½-in. brass mortars
- 30 4⅖-in. brass mortars
- 2 8-in. brass howitzers
- 4 5½-in. brass howitzers
- 26 24-pdr. brass battering cannons
- 12 18-pdr. brass battering cannons
- 6 6-pdr. light field pieces
- 15 iron ship's guns from Halifax

Total ordnance: 122

(Based mainly on Gordon's and Montresor's journals)

Royal Navy Ships at Louisbourg 1758

Vice-Admiral the Hon. Edward Boscawen, Officer Commanding

Rear-Admiral Sir Charles Hardy

HMS *Namur* 90 guns, 780 men
HMS *Royal William* 84 guns, 765 men
HMS *Princess Amelia* 80 guns, 665 men
HMS *Dublin* 74 guns, 600 men
HMS *Terrible* 74 guns, 600 men
HMS *Northumberland* 70 guns, 520 men
HMS *Oxford* 70 guns, 520 men
HMS *Vanguard* 70 guns, 520 men
HMS *Somerset* 70 guns, 520 men
HMS *Burford* 66 guns, 520 men
HMS *Lancaster* 66 guns, 520 men
HMS *Devonshire* 66 guns, 520 men
HMS *Bedford* 64 guns, 480 men
HMS *Prince Frederick* 64 guns, 480 men
HMS *Captain* 64 guns, 480 men
HMS *Nottingham* 60 guns, 400 men
HMS *Pembroke* 60 guns, 400 men
HMS *Kingston* 60 guns, 400 men
HMS *Prince of Orange* 60 guns, 400 men
HMS *York* 60 guns, 480 men
HMS *Defiance* 60 guns, 400 men
HMS *Sutherland* 50 guns, 350 men
HMS *Centurion* 50 guns, 350 men
HMS *Juno* 32 guns, 220 men
HMS *Diana* 32 guns, 220 men
HMS *Boreas* 28 guns, 200 men
HMS *Shannon* 28 guns, 200 men
HMS *Trent* 28 guns, 200 men
HMS *Hynd* 24 guns, 160 men
HMS *Portmabon* 24 guns, 160 men
HMS *Scarborough* 20 guns, 160 men
HMS *Nightingale* 20 guns, 160 men
HMS *Squirrel* 20 guns, 160 men
HMS *Kennington* 20 guns, 160 men
HMS *Grammont* 18 guns, 125 men
HMS *Hawke* 14 guns, 110 men
HMS *Hunter* 14 guns, 110 men
HMS *Aetna* 8 guns, 45 men
HMS *Lightning* 8 guns, 45 men
HMS *Tagloe*, 40 men

Total: 40 warships with 14,665 men. Assuming that one man in six was a marine, this included about 2,400 marines.

Officer, Grenadier Company, 60th Foot (Royal Americans), 1755–67. (Print after a reconstruction by P. W. Reynolds)

FRENCH ORDER OF BATTLE, JUNE 1758

Governor: Chevalier de Drucour
Commandant of the Troops: M. de la Houlière
Chief Engineer: Col. Louis Franquet
Commander of Naval Forces:
Commodore Jean-Antoine Charry, Marquis Desgouttes
Commissaire-Ordonnateur: Jacques Prévost de la Croix

Compagnies franches de la Marine (colonial infantry)
23 companies, about 90 officers and 800 enlisted men.
(Another company was on Isle Saint-Jean.)

Canonniers-Bombardiers (colonial artillery)
two companies, of about six officers and
100 enlisted men.

Artois Regiment, 2nd Bn.
about 32 officers and 520 enlisted men.

Bourgogne Regiment, 2nd Bn.
about 32 officers and 520 enlisted men.

Cambis Regiment, 2nd Bn
about 40 officers and 650 enlisted men.

Volontaires-Étrangers Regiment, 2nd Bn.
about 41 officers and 660 enlisted men.

Compagnies franches de la Marine (ship's marines)
about 10 officers and 150 enlisted men.

Total regular troops: about 3,450 enlisted men and about
251 officers. Total: about 3,690 all ranks. Bourgeois Militia,
about 300

Total: about 3,990 all ranks French land forces
within the town.

French Navy ships at Louisbourg 8 June – 26 July 1758

Le Prudent 74 guns, 680 men, burnt
L'Entreprenant 74 guns, 680 men, burnt
Le Capricieux 64 guns, 440 men, burnt
Le Célèbre 64 guns, 440 men, burnt
Le Bienfaisant 64 guns, 440 men, taken
L'Apollon 50 guns, 350 men, sunk
L'Aréthuse 36 guns, 270 men, escaped
Le Fidèle 36 guns, 270 men, sunk
La Chèvre 16 guns, 150 men, sunk
La Biche 16 guns, 150 men, sunk

Total: 10 warships with about 3,870 men. Assuming
that one man in six was a marine, this included about
645 marines. From 3 July, the men were landed except
for about 500 remaining on board the ships.

Grenadier, Cambis Regiment, c.1759–60. Note the
pre-regulation bearskin cap. French grenadiers officially
received bearskin caps with a brass plate in the lower front
following the regulations of 10 December 1762. (Royal
Library, Madrid)

THE LOUISBOURG GARRISON AT THE SURRENDER, 26 JULY 1758

24 companies colonial *Compagnies franches* and 2 companies of *Canonniers-Bombardiers*: 76 officers and 746 enlisted men fit for service, 195 sick and wounded, total: 1,017.

Artois Regiment: 32 officers and 407 enlisted men fit for service, 27 sick and wounded, total: 466.

Bourgogne Regiment: 30 officers and 353 enlisted men fit for service, 31 sick and wounded, total: 414.

Cambis Regiment: 38 officers and 466 enlisted men fit for service, 104 sick and wounded, total: 608.

Volontaires-Étrangers Regiment: 38 officers and 402 enlisted men fit for service, 86 sick and wounded, total: 526.

Total Garrison: 214 officers and 2,374 enlisted men fit for service, 443 sick and wounded, total: 3,031.

Naval officers, seamen and marines: 135 officers and 1,124 seamen and marines fit for service, 1,347 sick and wounded, total: 2,606.

Grand Total: 349 officers and 3,498 NCOs, privates and sailors fit for service, 1,790 sick and wounded, total: 5,637.

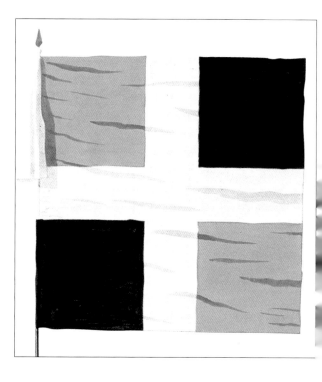

ABOVE **Battalion color, Artois Infantry Regiment, c. 1744–75. (Anne S. K. Brown Military Collection. Brown University)**

LEFT **Private, Cambis Infantry Regiment, c.1757. The lapels shown in this plate were probably never worn by the regiment. It is certain that the second battalion at Louisbourg did not have them. A detailed muster of the battalion embarking for Louisbourg describes the uniform as "White coat and breeches, red collar, cuffs and waistcoat, ordinary [horizontal] pocket with three buttons of which one is yellow and two white, the same quantity and colors on the cuff, hat lace of gold and silver." No lapels are mentioned, nor are they in the French army registers of the period. (Musée de l'Armée, Paris)**

THE LOUISBOURG CAMPAIGN OF 1758

NAVAL AND MILITARY PREPARATIONS

French naval strategy for the defense of Louisbourg in 1758 called for several squadrons to rendezvous at the port. Unlike 1757, however, the British were reinforced and more vigilant, while the French were somewhat weaker. A sizable squadron which included seven ships-of-the-line came out of Toulon but was soon chased by Admiral Osborne's strong Royal Navy squadron into taking refuge at Cartagena in Spain. The French Rochefort squadron comprised five ships-of-the-line and seven frigates to escort some 40 transport vessels assembled at Isle d'Aix. On 4 April, Admiral Edward Hawke's squadron caught up with them and chased them up the Charente River.

Effectively blockaded, there was not much the French could do except to slip out various ships in the hope that they would make a sufficiently strong squadron at Isle Royale. *Le Prudent* (74 guns), under Commodore the Marquis Desgouttes, arrived on 24 March. Four days

ISLE ROYALE: EARLY JUNE 1758

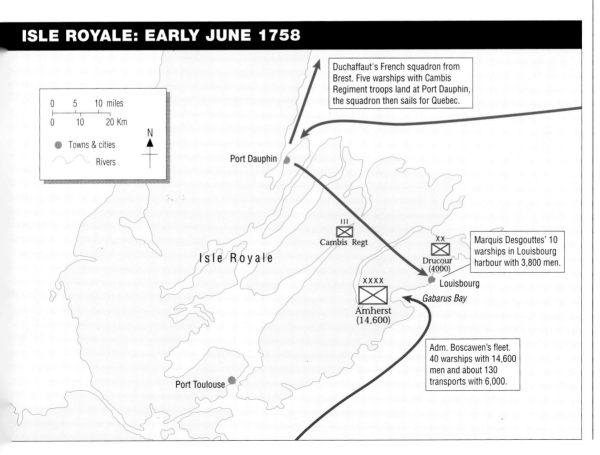

0 5   10 miles
0   10   20 Km

N

● Towns & cities
〜 Rivers

Duchaffaut's French squadron from Brest. Five warships with Cambis Regiment troops land at Port Dauphin, the squadron then sails for Quebec.

Port Dauphin

III
Cambis Regt

Isle Royale

XX
Drucour
(4000)

Marquis Desgouttes' 10 warships in Louisbourg harbour with 3,800 men.

Louisbourg

Gabarus Bay

XXXX
Amherst
(14,600)

Adm. Boscawen's fleet. 40 warships with 14,600 men and about 130 transports with 6,000.

Port Toulouse

later, Commodore Beaussier de L'Isle came in with *L'Entreprenant* (74 guns), *Le Capricieux* (64 guns), *Le Célèbre* (64 guns), *Le Bienfaisant* (64 guns) and *La Comète* (32 guns). But the last three ships were fitted as transports and carried the second battalion of the *Volontaires-Étrangers* Regiment to reinforce the garrison. *L'Apollon* (50 guns), *L'Aréthuse* (36 guns), *La Fidèle* (36 guns), *La Chèvre* (16 guns), *L'Echo* (32 guns) and *La Biche* (16 guns) trickled in with a few transports during April and May.

The only sizable French squadron to leave Brest for Isle Royale was under Commodore Duchaffault. It was also the last, and consisted of: *Le Tonnant* (80 guns), *L'Intrépide* (74 guns), *Le Héros* (74 guns), *La Prothée* (64 guns) and *La Belliqueuse* (64 guns). It did not come into Louisbourg but, in early June, landed the second battalion of the Cambis Regiment at Port Dauphin, then headed for Quebec. Meanwhile, on the southern side of the island, Admiral Boscawen's fleet was advancing.

THE SUPERIORITY OF THE BRITISH FORCES

This time, there was no doubt that the Royal Navy had total superiority over the French fleet in North America and, indeed, on the North Atlantic. Admiral Boscawen's fleet assembled in Halifax numbered some 23 ships-of-the-line, 18 frigates and smaller vessels manned by about 14,600 sailors and marines. They escorted about 127 transport vessels which carried about 5,000 – 6,000 merchant sailors. They were ready to take on board some 13,000 troops, as well as a train of siege artillery and all manners of supplies. The French had nothing to oppose such a gathering, and it was clear that this time, Louisbourg would indeed come under siege.

The numerous land and sea forces gathering in Halifax were in great spirits. Gone was the gloom which had overshadowed the previous year's attempt. The mood amongst the expedition's officers was obviously optimistic. Wolfe gave a dinner on 24 May, and the 47 officers dining at the Great Pontac hotel in Halifax that night would have included Boscawen, Lawrence, Whitmore, Bastide, Robert Monkton, who was acting as governor of Nova Scotia, Col. William Howe, Lord Rollo, and many others. Between them, they washed down their meal with some 70 bottles of Madeira, 50 bottles of claret and 25 bottles of brandy – averaging over three bottles per guest – to the music of ten musicians, the whole costing Wolfe nearly £100. The future conqueror of Quebec, by no means a great drinker, had a bon vivant side to his personality and was fond of asking: "How stands the glass around?" Sadly, Amherst missed the dinner as he was had not yet arrived in Halifax but it must have been a convivial mess evening, full of cheerful optimism and warlike toasts.

RIGHT **Officer and privates of British Marines, c. 1755–60. The marines wore miter caps that were somewhat smaller than those of infantry grenadiers. (Print after a reconstruction by V. Huen)**

BELOW **Battalion color, *Volontaires-Étrangers* Regiment, 1756–59. The cross was white with quarters half green and half white. (Musée de l'Armée, Paris)**

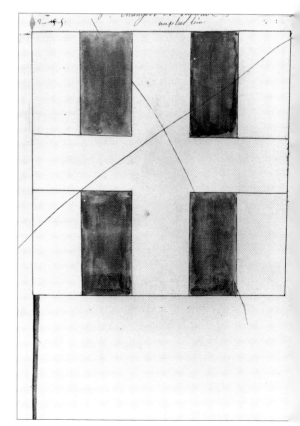

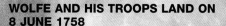

WOLFE AND HIS TROOPS LAND ON 8 JUNE 1758

After six days of frustrated attempts, both by the bad weather and the French shore defenses, the British launched a general landing assault on 8 June 1758 at Cormorandière (now Kennington) Cove. Of the three British landing divisions, Brig. Gen. Wolfe's light infantrymen finally managed to set foot on the rocky shore of a relatively undefended area in spite of the heavy surf. Soon, Wolfe himself was there leading on his grenadiers as shown in the painting. Wolfe probably wore the all-red campaign dress he favoured. The grenadiers shown are mostly from the 40th Foot and the 78th Highlanders, but companies from all regiments in the expedition landed with Wolfe's division. The longboats are taken from models at the National Army Museum. Securing this beachhead was a most important event in the Louisbourg campaign and was far from a foregone conclusion considering the difficult terrain, the French shore defenses and the persistently bad weather that plagued the British fleet.

THE SIEGE DAY BY DAY

The siege of Louisbourg, like most any large-scale siege, was very much a day-by-day affair which went on for weeks. In the case of Louisbourg, it took seven weeks from the British arrival at Louisbourg to the surrender. Thus the following account is a daily report taken and summarized from the journals of several participants on both sides, notably Amherst, Drucour, Montresor, Gordon, ships' logs and several anonymous accounts. The events and even the dates of the events are sometimes in conflict from one journal to the next. In such cases, we have used the journals of the commanders as the reference.

28 May Boscawen's armada sailed from Halifax and was joined by a few more sloops and schooners.

2 June The British fleet was in the Louisbourg area and HMS *Namur* had reckoned the western point of Gabarus Bay. The winds, which had been strong, were lessening, but fog and drizzling rain set in as the fleet gathered in Gabarus Bay. French detachments were posted all along the coast watching the ships sailing "in two files" according to Drucour. To reinforce the garrison, Desgouttes sent 100 sailors to serve in the town.

3 June The British fleet weighed anchor in Gabarus Bay. HMS *Namur*'s boats were hoisted out "and the Generals went to reconnoiter the coast." Amherst decided to try landing the next day. The landing troops would be divided into three groups under brigadiers Wolfe, Lawrence and Whitmore. In the evening, the French on shore fired a rocket and a gun, no doubt as a signal to the town.

4 June Several British ships came close to shore and "began to fire on ye enemy," but no landing was attempted due to bad weather. In

Cormorandière (or Kennington) Cove from a 1912 photo.

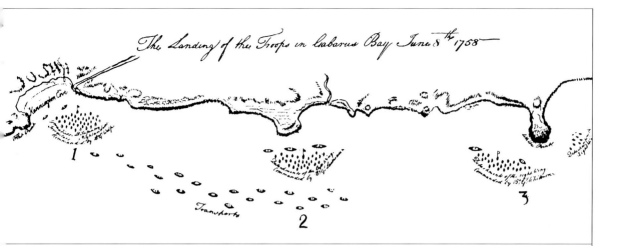

The Landing of the Troops in Gabarus Bay June 8th 1758

The British landing succeeded on 8 June at Cormorandière (or Kennington) Cove thanks to Wolfe's mixed force of grenadiers, light infantry and Highlanders. The troops were divided into three groups under (1) Wolfe at left, (2) Lawrence, and (3) Whitmore.

Louisbourg, another 250 sailors from Desgouttes' fleet were landed to reinforce the garrison. Fog and strong winds continued to hamper the British for the next several days making landing attempts impossible.

6 June At noon, ten companies of the Cambis Regiment marched into Louisbourg. They had been landed at Port Dauphin from Commodore Duchaffault's small French squadron, which then sailed on to Quebec. At this time, some 2,005 men, which was most of the garrison, were posted outside the walls.

7 June Fog and a heavy surf prevented a landing by the British. In the evening, however, the weather calmed a bit and Amherst ordered a landing attempt early the next morning.

THE BRITISH SECURE BEACHHEAD

8 June At 4 am, the weather being at last rather good, the British decided to attempt a general landing at Cormorandière Cove and a rocket was fired as a signal. The boats were filled with soldiers and rowed towards the shore in a wavy sea, while warships bombarded the shore defenses. The initial attempt at landing was repulsed by the French, who waited until the boats were in the cove to open a cross fire with a 24-pdr., four 6-pdrs., and musketry fire from the French infantry "that had lined the whole bay, and were covered by a breast work." To make matters worse, the wind rose again and made "the surf so great that the troops could not get on shore," noted Amherst. Things were going badly, with boats full of troops all over the bay caught in a rough surf, being fired upon, and unable to land.

In one of the boats was young Brig. Gen. Wolfe leading the Left Division, consisting of the grenadier companies, the light infantry, the rangers, and the 78th. Searching for a solution, he ordered his boats to row further left of the cove. It worked, and a boatload of light infantry under lieutenants Brown and Hopkins landed in spite of the surf "with the utmost difficulty" and scrambled up the rocks at Anse-aux-Sables, a small cove full of rocks overlooked by a steep bluff. Wolfe directed as many boats to it as fast as possible to support the men already on shore, then, armed only with a cane, he jumped in the surf and waded on shore with the Highlanders and grenadiers. All this was done at great risk, as Amherst saw them "in a violent surf, several of the boats overturning and

49

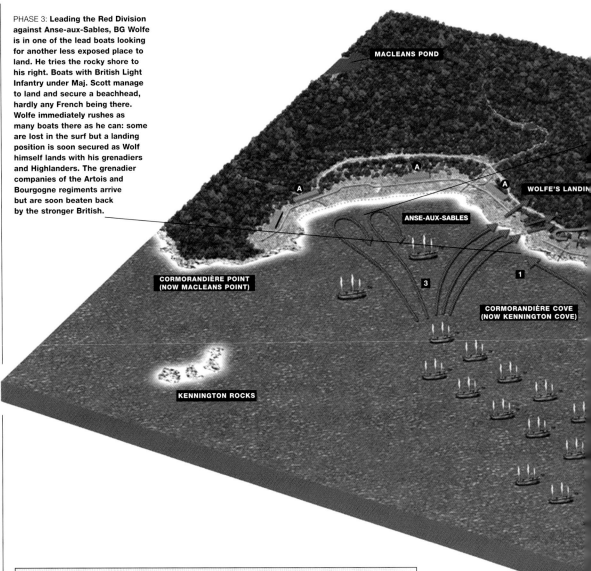

PHASE 3: Leading the Red Division against Anse-aux-Sables, BG Wolfe is in one of the lead boats looking for another less exposed place to land. He tries the rocky shore to his right. Boats with British Light Infantry under Maj. Scott manage to land and secure a beachhead, hardly any French being there. Wolfe immediately rushes as many boats there as he can: some are lost in the surf but a landing position is soon secured as Wolf himself lands with his grenadiers and Highlanders. The grenadier companies of the Artois and Bourgogne regiments arrive but are soon beaten back by the stronger British.

MACLEANS POND

A

A

A

WOLFE'S LANDIN

ANSE-AUX-SABLES

CORMORANDIÈRE POINT
(NOW MACLEANS POINT)

3

1

CORMORANDIÈRE COVE
(NOW KENNINGTON COVE)

KENNINGTON ROCKS

FRENCH UNITS

The area of Cormorandière (later Kennington) Cove was previously fortified with various field works. The works given in this bird's-eye view are largely after a plan of 1757 as no detailed plan of the 1758 works appears to exist. The situation in June 1758 seems much the same as previously. The beach areas of Anse-aux-Sables and Anse-aux-Ruisseau were covered with abbatis. A very lengthy parapet of earth with fascines bordered the shore above the beaches and rocks. Four six-pounders were mounted, two at Anse-aux-Sables and two at Anse-aux-Ruisseau, with a few swivel guns as well as 24-pounder at an uncertain locale.

A The French units are not specified apart from the grenadiers of Artois and Bourgogne. Of the 2,000 men posted in various works outside, Drucour reported 985 men under Lt. Col. Saint-Julien of the Artois Regiment in the Cormorandière area. It thus would appear the units at Cormorandière were Artois and Bourgogne but there may have been detachments from other units. For instance, a few gunners of the *Canonniers-Bombardiers* would have served the guns.

B Grenadier companies of Artois and Bourgogne.

BRITISH UNITS

1 **The Red Division (BG Wolfe)**
Grenadier companies of all regiments (those of the 1st, 15th, 17th and 22nd with Wolfe). Light Infantry and one company of rangers. 78th Highlanders.

2 **The Blue Division (BG Lawrence)**
15th
22nd
35th
40th
45th
3/60th

3 **The White Division (BG Whitmore)**
2/1st
17th
47th
48th
58th
2/60th

XX

WOLFE

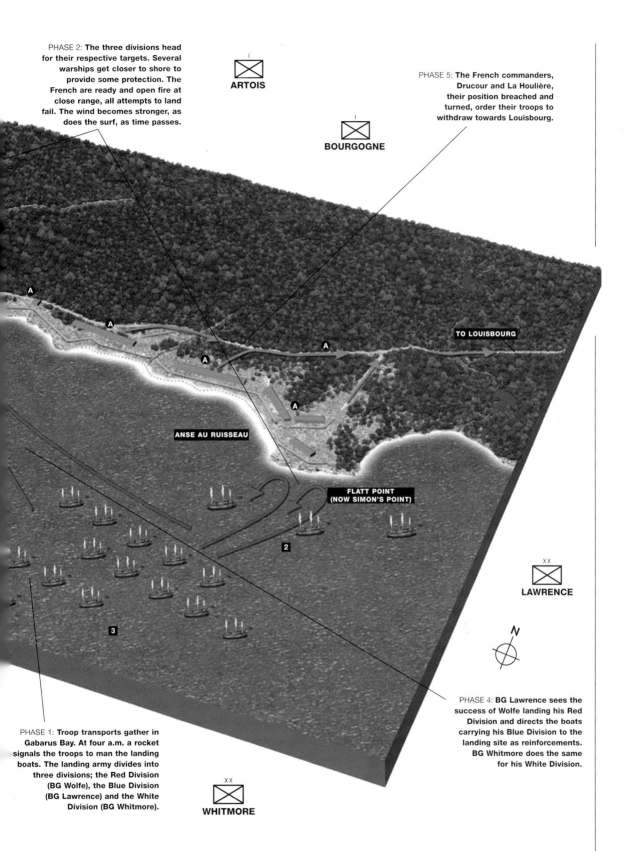

PHASE 2: **The three divisions head for their respective targets. Several warships get closer to shore to provide some protection. The French are ready and open fire at close range, all attempts to land fail. The wind becomes stronger, as does the surf, as time passes.**

ARTOIS

BOURGOGNE

PHASE 5: **The French commanders, Drucour and La Houlière, their position breached and turned, order their troops to withdraw towards Louisbourg.**

A

A

A

A

TO LOUISBOURG

A

ANSE AU RUISSEAU

A

**FLATT POINT
(NOW SIMON'S POINT)**

2

LAWRENCE

X X

N

3

PHASE 4: **BG Lawrence sees the success of Wolfe landing his Red Division and directs the boats carrying his Blue Division to the landing site as reinforcements. BG Whitmore does the same for his White Division.**

PHASE 1: **Troop transports gather in Gabarus Bay. At four a.m. a rocket signals the troops to man the landing boats. The landing army divides into three divisions; the Red Division (BG Wolfe), the Blue Division (BG Lawrence) and the White Division (BG Whitmore).**

WHITMORE

X X

3 JUNE 1758: WOLFE SECURES A BEACHHEAD

all the men jumping in the water to get on shore." They were fired at by a few French soldiers in the area, but the British soon consolidated their position.

The French had not considered a landing likely at Anse-aux-Sables and had not built extensive defenses or posted many men in that area. It was not negligence, but simply because they did not have enough men to guard an area as large as Gabarus Bay. Grenadier companies were stationed as reserves at intervals should a landing occur. It was hoped they could push back to the sea the small parties that might land. The French saw Wolfe's men land and the grenadier companies of Artois and Bourgogne arrived to reinforce the piquet, but it was already too late. Hundreds of British troops had landed within minutes. When Wolfe saw the French come up, he coolly formed up his men in rank to return a withering fire, killing the captain and the sub-lieutenant of Bourgogne's grenadier company. The French grenadiers retreated with their wounded. Meanwhile, Whitmore's and Lawrence's divisions went to Wolfe's landing place, and the beachhead was soon totally secured.

The French position had been turned and their retreat was inevitable. Wolfe's men engaged further French troops, and stormed and took a shore battery at bayonet point, while other British brigades were rushing to join them. Within half an hour, some 4,000–5,000 men stepped ashore. Pressed by Wolfe's troops, Drucour and de la Houlière ordered the withdrawal of their men back to Louisbourg. They now rightly feared that the French troops still posted at Cormorandière Cove might be cut off. The retreat was effected in good order, although they

Wolfe lands with his troops under fire at Louisbourg on 8 June 1758. The rough seas dashed them against the shore's rocks in a scene very different from the relatively calm sea and flat landscape shown in this print after J. Macfarlane.

The King's Bastion is seen in the distance from across the marshes and brush to the south. This would have been the view seen by British scouts marching from the White Point area.

had to abandon the guns at the shore batteries, which were now useless anyway. British parties followed them but stopped when they got within artillery range of the town's bastions, which opened up a tremendous fire. By noon, the action was over. The landing had been successful, but it was clear that a full-scale siege would have to be undertaken. The British reported two officers and 37 men killed and 18 men wounded. Drucour noted two officers killed and one wounded but did not mention the casualties of the enlisted men. The British thought they had killed over 100 French, which seems a considerable exaggeration, as an anonymous French journal reported confirmed that they retreated into the city in good order and only had "a loss of 18 soldiers" (PRO, WO 34/101).

In the evening, the rest of the Cambis Regiment arrived in town. Meanwhile, *Le Bizarre* and *Le Comète* safely slipped out of the harbor.

9–11 June In spite of bad weather, the British established a large camp at Gabarus with a perimeter of field works to consolidate their beachhead. French scouts reported to Drucour and his officers that the British were solidly entrenched in great numbers, perhaps as many as 12,000 men having landed, which was remarkably accurate intelligence.

WOLFE TAKES LIGHTHOUSE POINT

12 June With a strong force of about 1,400 men, including four companies of grenadiers, Wolfe left the camp at 4 am. Their objective was to capture Lighthouse Point on the other side of the town. This required a long march through unfamiliar terrain from Gabarus all the way around the harbor to get up to the lighthouse. There was always the possibility of being ambushed by parties of Canadians, Acadians and Indians but the British must have noted there was no sign of them in the vicinity. Maj. Ross was posted with 400 men at the far end of the harbor, to the north-east, with orders to entrench. Wolfe and the rest of his force went on. By 2 pm, they had reached Lighthouse Point and immediately established a camp. The small French battery near the lighthouse had previously been abandoned and its cannons thrown over the cliff.

53

In the afternoon, French volunteers skirmished with British light infantrymen south of the town and spiked two cannons at a battery near White Point. The French later noticed "a lot of people" near the lighthouse and the Island Battery and fired a few shots at them.

13 June At about 9 am, Gen. Wolfe received a message from Maj. Ross that three parties of French troops were advancing towards his entrenched position. Wolfe sent the four grenadier companies to support him, but the French did not attack and retired after burning down a few buildings in the area to prevent the British using them.

The troops in the main British camp were busy erecting magazines and field hospitals. Supplies were still being landed but the heavy surf made this difficult. Gen. Amherst wanted to secure the heights overlooking the landing site with three redoubts. Accordingly, a strong detachment went out to carry out the order, but at about 11 am, ran into a strong force of some 300 French troops posted in the area and much shooting ensued. As more and more British troops were coming out of the camp to reinforce their comrades, the French were overwhelmed and forced to retreat. It was a lively two-hour fight, the French reporting one officer seriously wounded. The British lost a lieutenant and a soldier killed and six men wounded while two deserters from *Volontaires-Étrangers* claimed the French had five killed and 40 wounded, a total that seems rather high.

Meanwhile, the French gunners in the Island Battery trained some of their guns on Wolfe's position at Lighthouse Point. Their fire soon gave cause for concern and, at 9 pm, the tents were struck and moved away to a covered position.

The frigate *L'Echo* sailed out of Louisbourg bound for Quebec, but was chased and eventually captured by HMS *Juno*.

Louisbourg seen in the distance from about halfway up the hills to the north-west. This would be what British scouts and Wolfe first saw of Louisbourg in June 1758.

14 June Several British transport vessels anchored in a small cove near Wolfe's camp at Lighthouse Point to unload supplies. In spite of the heavy surf, this did not go unnoticed by the French gunners on Battery Island, who opened fire on the transports and were joined by a small French gunboat armed with two 24-pdrs. The British frigates HMS *Hunter* and HMS *Diana* were in the vicinity and returned fire, but were soon damaged when the powerful French battery found their range. The engagement ended in a draw, with the transport ships able to unload fascines and artillery.

On the west side, Amherst continued to build three redoubts and moved more troops closer to the town. The French volunteer company on the heights overlooking the Dauphin Gate had to retreat.

15–16 June The British objective was to put some gun positions on Lighthouse Point and at other locations at the far end of the harbor to bombard the French ships. Governor Drucour's decision to demolish the Royal Battery before the siege began was sensible, as its capture would have provided the British with a powerful strongpoint that commanded the inner harbor. The British now had to build their siege works and spent the next two days erecting batteries while the French warships in the harbor fired broadsides at them. They probably looked and sounded impressive but do not seem to have been very effective, probably due to the distance. On the 16th, however, the French on the Island Battery killed three men and wounded five British soldiers at Lighthouse Point.

17 June Gen. Amherst held a meeting near the demolished Royal Battery with the engineers Bastide, MacKellar, and Williamson. It was their opinion that the Green Hill, west of the town, should be secured and a road built to reach it. The Royal Navy were unable enter the harbor to deal with the French fleet that constantly fired at anything that moved on the harbor shores, so it would be necessary to reinforce the battery at Lighthouse Point with five mortars as "the Island Battery must be destroyed from that side if the Shipping [Royal Navy warships] may not assist us," according to Amherst.

Under a flag of truce, Gen. Amherst also had two pineapples, then a rare delicacy, sent to Madame de Drucour with his regrets concerning the inconveniences the circumstances of war would cause her.

18 June The French noted that communications between the British camp at Gabarus and the batteries under construction at the end of the harbor seemed constant, but no cannons seemed yet installed. British deserters confirmed that the army besieging Louisbourg had about 12,000 soldiers mostly from Britain, except for a "corps of 1,600 men from New England, soldiers not in uniform" according to Drucour. This was Howe's corps which was actually British light infantry and New England rangers combined, about 1,050 men.

At about 2 pm, the Marquis Desgouttes sent a boat under a flag of truce at the end of the harbor with 50 bottles of wine from Madame de Drucour in acknowledgment of Gen. Amherst's kindness.

THE BOMBARDMENTS BEGIN

19 June From this date, the siege entered a bombardment phase which it maintained until the end. Howitzers had been added to the cannons and mortars, and 24-pdrs. were still being landed from the fleet. The British harbor batteries were now just about ready in spite of the shelling from Desgouttes' ships. As the evening set in, Gen. Wolfe, who commanded the area, now ordered the new batteries to open up and return the French ships' fire. The French saw a number of fires lit along the coast and on the heights west of the town, then saw signals with rockets. A short while later, the British "started bombarding the ships in the harbor and fired about 120 bombs, one of which fell on board *Le Prudent*, wounding several sailors, and others exploding in the air over the masts" (Drucour).

20 June In the evening, the British battery at Lighthouse Point, which now had mortars, started shelling the French on Battery Island. A furious artillery began and continued the next day. The French battery further back at Rochefort Point, was also active, but the exchange was mainly between Battery Island and Lighthouse Point as the two were almost face to face. The British commanders saw that to succeed, Battery Island simply had to be "silenced" and, on the 22nd, some 400 men were sent to Lighthouse Point to build up the existing gun positions into a large battery, capable of doing the job. It took another three days and nights of work to finish the job, the soldiers constantly menaced by the French artillery fire. The French demonstrated remarkably good gunnery; they were at a disadvantage as they were situated at sea level and had to shoot at a battery high on a cliff.

21–24 June The French ships in the harbor moved nearer to the town on the 21st. The weather on 22 June was "most terrible" according to Amherst, while Boscawen reported having lost

Charles Deschamps de Boishébert (1727–97) became a cadet in the Canadian colonial troops aged 12, was commissioned in 1742, and promoted lieutenant in 1748. From 1744, he participated in expeditions in the wilderness, quickly developing skills as an outstanding bush warfare tactician. During his first expedition to Acadia in 1746, he helped repulse a British attack on Isle Saint-Jean and took part in the highly successful raid on Grand Pré the following year. Thereafter, he commanded mixed parties of Acadians, Canadians, and Indians in the area of the St John River (New Brunswick) keeping the British in western Nova Scotia on their toes. Hampered by a lack of supplies, he could do little with his small force against Amherst's huge army during the 1758 siege. A handsome man, he was called "le beau Canadien" by the Acadians. After the fall of Canada, he married and settled down in France.

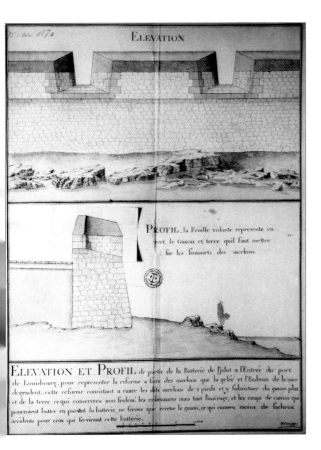

ELEVATION

PROFIL. la Feuille volante represente en
vert le Gazon et terre quil faut mettre
fur les fommets des merlons.

ELEVATION ET PROFIL de partie de la Batterie de l'islot a l'Entrée du port
de Louisbourg, pour representer la reforme a faire des merlons que la gelée et l'Embrun de la mer
degradent, cette reforme consistant a razer les dits merlons de 2 pieds et y fubsituer du gazon plat
et de la terre, ce qui conservera non feulem! les embrazures mais tout l'ouvrage, et les coups de canon qui
pourroient battre en passant la batterie ne feront que écreter le gazon, ce qui caussera moins de facheux
accidents pour ceux qui serviront cette batterie.

The tops of the Island Battery's crenellated walls were damaged by frost and the sea over the years. This 1735 plan shows changes to protect the tops with earth covered with grass to better resist the elements. Archives Nationales, Dépôt des Fortifications des Colonies)

over 100 boats to the very heavy surf while trying to land troops and supplies. The weather improved the next day and more artillery was landed. Meanwhile, the Island Battery and the French ships in the harbor kept up their bombardment and "threw a good many shots into the Camp." On 23 June, Drucour received word that Boishébert had arrived at Miramichi on 8 June and was marching towards Louisbourg with a mixed force of colonial troops, militiamen, and Micmac Indians.

On the 24th the weather was fine, and at 10 am a British drummer under a flag of truce took a dispatch concerning prisoners to Drucour from Amherst. He also sent two more pineapples for Madame Drucour. This time, she thanked the drummer with a handsome tip but did not send wine. As Governor Drucour put it, the British general seemingly wanted to exchange "my wine cellar for pineapples."

25 June The Lighthouse Point battery had eight heavy siege guns besides the mortars which, from their position on a height, had a good command of Battery Island and fired at it all day. The British were in a far better position and the French guns were raked by damaging fire. During the bombardment, a French "brass mortar was dismounted [from its carriage] and broken by a cannonball that went into [its chamber] and provoked the explosion of its bomb" (Drucour). By the evening, Battery Island's guns were reduced to silence. Several bombs landed on the magazines and the gun platforms and three embrasures were destroyed. Luckily for the French, only five or six gunners were wounded and none killed.

On the other side of town, Amherst wanted to occupy Green Hill. The engineers objected saying that more fascines and gabions should be put up on the road approaching the hill to protect the troops, as the French "fired a good deal" and Amherst agreed.

WOLFE TAKES GREEN HILL

26 June Although the Island Battery had been silenced the previous evening, the British battery at Lighthouse Point kept bombarding it through the night. Drucour was not about to give up, and had the guns and mortars installed on the Queen's, the King's, and the Dauphin bastions fire at the approaching British positions to the south and west.

The next step for the British was to successively occupy the heights around the harbor, with Amherst "resolved to take hold of Green Hill." Leading four companies of grenadiers and 200 fusiliers, Gen. Wolfe occupied a height evacuated by the French. Some French troops made a sortie heading towards the British light infantry camp, but ran into

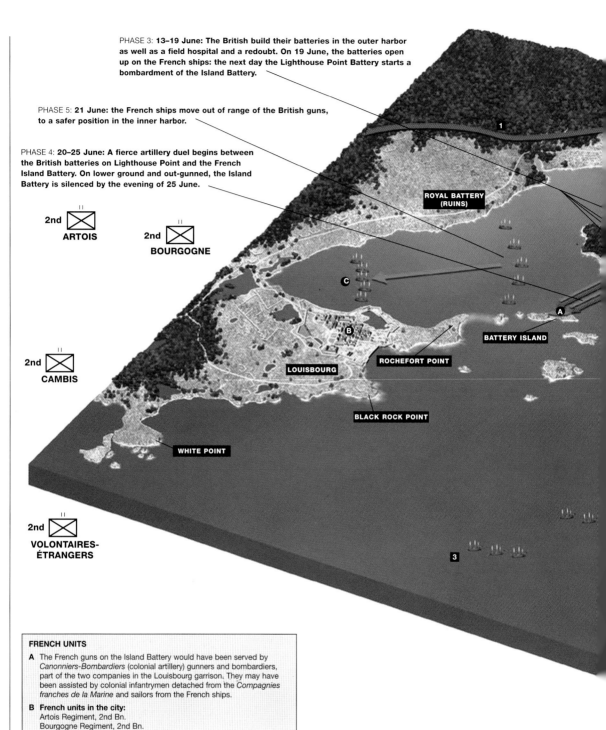

PHASE 3: **13–19 June: The British build their batteries in the outer harbor as well as a field hospital and a redoubt. On 19 June, the batteries open up on the French ships: the next day the Lighthouse Point Battery starts a bombardment of the Island Battery.**

PHASE 5: **21 June: the French ships move out of range of the British guns, to a safer position in the inner harbor.**

PHASE 4: **20–25 June: A fierce artillery duel begins between the British batteries on Lighthouse Point and the French Island Battery. On lower ground and out-gunned, the Island Battery is silenced by the evening of 25 June.**

2nd **ARTOIS**

2nd **BOURGOGNE**

2nd **CAMBIS**

2nd **VOLONTAIRES-ÉTRANGERS**

ROYAL BATTERY (RUINS)

Ⓒ

Ⓑ

Ⓐ

BATTERY ISLAND

ROCHEFORT POINT

LOUISBOURG

BLACK ROCK POINT

WHITE POINT

1

3

2nd

FRENCH UNITS

A The French guns on the Island Battery would have been served by *Canonniers-Bombardiers* (colonial artillery) gunners and bombardiers, part of the two companies in the Louisbourg garrison. They may have been assisted by colonial infantrymen detached from the *Compagnies franches de la Marine* and sailors from the French ships.

B French units in the city:
Artois Regiment, 2nd Bn.
Bourgogne Regiment, 2nd Bn.
Cambis Regiment, 2nd Bn.
Volontaires-Étrangers Regiment, 2nd Bn.
Compagnies franches de la Marine (colonial infantry).
Canonniers-Bombardiers (colonial artillery).
Bourgeois Militia.
Compagnies franches de la Marine (about 150 metropolitan marines detached from ships).

C French ships:
Bienfaisant.
Prudent.
Entreprenant.
Célèbre.
Capricieux.

BRITISH UNITS
1 Wolfe's Corps on 12 June included grenadiers of 1st, 15th, 17th and 22nd regiments, ten men per company from each regiment, light infantry and rangers.

2 Engineers with infantrymen acting as pioneers build batteries. The Royal Artillery serves the guns, assisted by detached infantrymen.

3 Royal Navy ships blockade the harbor.

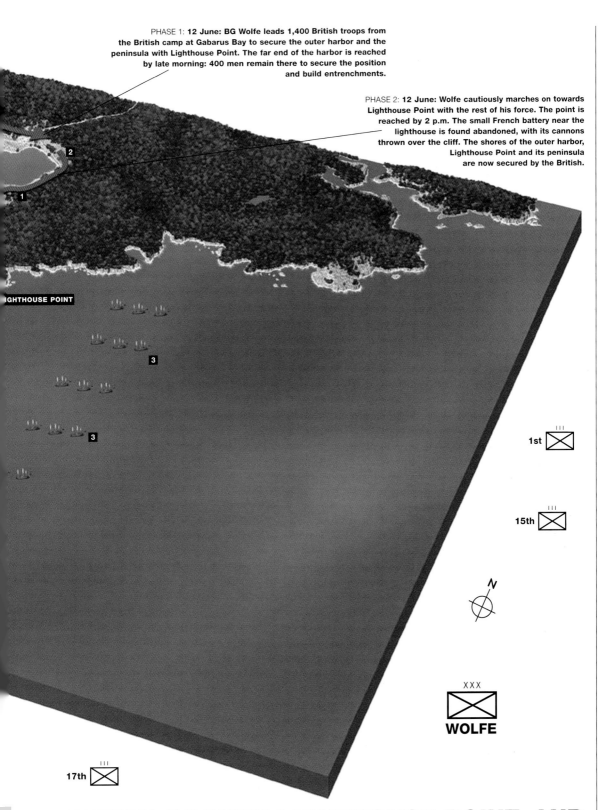

PHASE 1: **12 June**: BG Wolfe leads 1,400 British troops from the British camp at Gabarus Bay to secure the outer harbor and the peninsula with Lighthouse Point. The far end of the harbor is reached by late morning: 400 men remain there to secure the position and build entrenchments.

PHASE 2: **12 June**: Wolfe cautiously marches on towards Lighthouse Point with the rest of his force. The point is reached by 2 p.m. The small French battery near the lighthouse is found abandoned, with its cannons thrown over the cliff. The shores of the outer harbor, Lighthouse Point and its peninsula are now secured by the British.

LIGHTHOUSE POINT

1st

15th

N

XXX
WOLFE

17th

HE BRITISH OCCUPY LIGHTHOUSE POINT, AND BOMBARD BATTERY ISLAND, 12–25 JUNE 1758

William Amherst, detached from the 1st Foot Guards, served as ADC to his elder brother Jeffery, who commanded the British forces during the siege of Louisbourg. He left a remarkable journal of the siege. (Print after a c.1770 portrait)

forward posts of the Left Brigade and the light infantrymen. The outnumbered French withdrew into the town. The British wished to press their advantage and, in the evening, they secured Green Hill, which was just 900 meters west of the Dauphin Bastion and gate. Wolfe was the senior commander in that area

27–28 June The occupation of Green Hill by the British was bad news for the French. They reasoned that, sooner or later, Green Hill would be transformed into a strong British position that would threaten the town's west side. On 27 June, the heavy guns in the Dauphin Bastion opened up a brisk fire at the British on Green Hill. The French noted that each shot "obliged the enemy to abandon their post to hide or go away." The British soldiers thus sheltered themselves as best they could while trying to build up the works.

On 28 June, the French frigate *L'Aréthuse* came closer and fired flanking broadsides at workers who were trying to build up a protective "epaulement" earthen wall along the road leading from Green Hill to the city's Dauphin Gate to make a covert-way. The work at the road was interrupted, and the men withdrew to Green Hill.

29–30 June The next couple of days were very dangerous for the British pioneers and soldiers working on the batteries. The French warships in the harbor and the town's batteries poured a relentless fire which often caused considerable disturbances, as Drucour noted. But the British were not about to be discouraged, and the work went on in spite of being "very heavy and tedious" according to Amherst. Slowly but surely the British batteries were erected and gradually provided better and better protection as time passed.

With the Island Battery out of action, the possibility that the British squadron "flying the standard with the cross of St George" (the White Ensign) might break into the harbor was very real. To prevent this, Drucour and Desgouttes agreed to scuttle ships at the entrance. On the night of 28 to 29 June, *L'Apollon*, *Le Fidèle*, *La Chèvre* and *La Biche* were sacrificed. *Le Prudent*, *L'Entreprenant*, *Le Capricieux*, *Le Célèbre*, *Le Bienfaisant* and *L'Aréthuse* still remained in the harbor, with *L'Aréthuse* reportedly firing some 100 rounds at the British working in the Green Hill area on the night of the 30th.

On 29–30 June, a small group of Indians was seen near Cormorandière Cove. They were pursued and, according to William Amherst (ADC to his older brother, Jeffery), "two were killed and their scalps brought in." This was an isolated party, not part of Boishébert's force, which had not yet reached the area.

1 July In the early morning, two French piquets and two companies of volunteers, a force totaling about 200 men, slipped out of the town to get wood to the north. The British were vigilant and saw the move

Scott's light infantry with some Highlanders of the 78th engaged them. Amherst immediately sent some 400 men (two companies of grenadiers from the 28th and the 48th, and six pickets) to support Wolfe. The British turned the situation to their advantage and gained possession of two small heights nearer to the town. Wolfe led four companies of grenadiers which occupied the height nearest to the Dauphin Bastion. He was soon joined by two more companies to secure the position. After about an hour and a half of skirmish shooting, the French retreated back to town as Murray's reserves were arriving. This was an opportunity Amherst quickly exploited by sending 200 pioneers to dig into the new forward position with three pickets to cover them.

On the other side of town, two French piquets went towards White Point to demolish fascines and *chevaux-de-frises*. Again, the British were vigilant and sent a strong force, estimated at 300 men by the French, to drive the piquets back after an hour of skirmishing.

Drucour also reported that the British gunners serving in the battery at Lighthouse Point had managed to find the town's range, in spite of the distance, as several cannonballs from its 24- and 32-pounders crashed into the city.

2 July The British immediately decided to build a large semicircular defense on the height they had just taken near the Dauphin Gate, and called it Grenadiers' Redoubt. It was in an excellent position to batter down the fortifications on the west side of the city. The French knew it, and also realized that they were in no position to recapture it. Drucour reported that his parties of volunteers could hardly operate outside the city any longer. Given their resources, the best they could do was to cannonade the British troops working on this new redoubt both from the town and from the warships in the harbor. On the British side, work went on in earnest, each soldier understanding the critical importance of this building work in spite of the great personal danger.

3 July Boishébert's detachment reached the vicinity of Louisbourg but this mixed body of Canadians, Acadians and Indians was in a miserable state. The supplies they had expected Drucour to send to Miramichi were not there and the force, which was smaller than the 500 men expected, was too short of food and equipment to be fully effective.

Lighthouse Point and the Island Battery were separated by only a third of a mile. The dominating height of Lighthouse Point ensured that a battery installed on it would "silence" the Island Battery, as it indeed did in 1758. However, the harbor remained blocked as the French scuttled *l'Apollon* in the narrow entrance. (Detail from Jefferys' map)

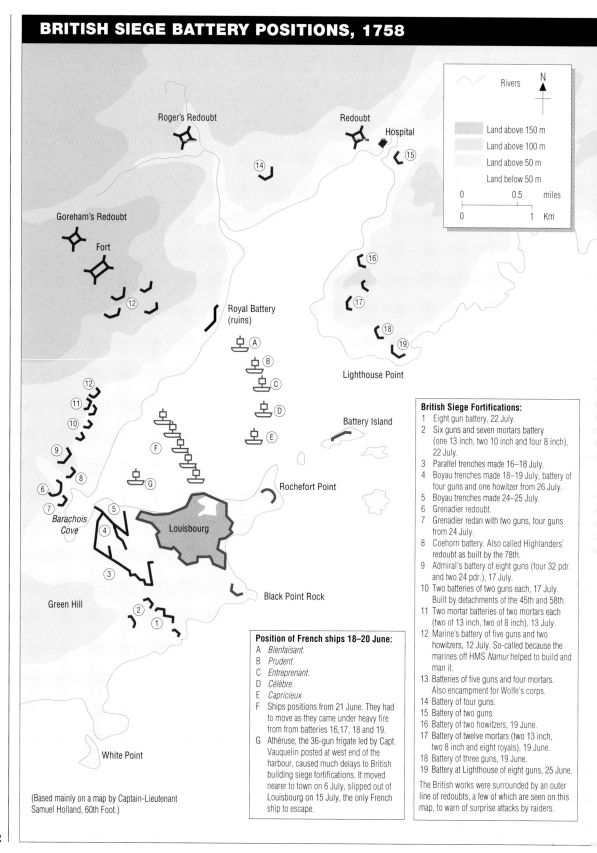

Rivers

N

Land above 150 m
Land above 100 m
Land above 50 m
Land below 50 m

0   0.5   miles
0   1   Km

Roger's Redoubt

Redoubt

Hospital

14

15

Goreham's Redoubt

Fort

16

12

17

Royal Battery
(ruins)

18

19

Lighthouse Point

A

B

C

D

Battery Island

12

11

E

10

F

9

8

G

6

Rochefort Point

7

*Barachois
Cove*

5

Louisbourg

4

3

Black Point Rock

Green Hill

2

1

White Point

(Based mainly on a map by Captain-Lieutenant
Samuel Holland, 60th Foot.)

Position of French ships 18–20 June:
A *Bienfaisant.*
B *Prudent.*
C *Entreprenant.*
D *Célèbre.*
E *Capricieux*
F Ships positions from 21 June. They had
   to move as they came under heavy fire
   from from batteries 16,17, 18 and 19.
G *Athéruse,* the 36-gun frigate led by Capt.
   Vauquelin posted at west end of the
   harbour, caused much delays to British
   building siege fortifications. It moved
   nearer to town on 6 July, slipped out of
   Louisbourg on 15 July, the only French
   ship to escape.

British Siege Fortifications:
1 Eight gun battery, 22 July.
2 Six guns and seven mortars battery
   (one 13 inch, two 10 inch and four 8 inch),
   22 July.
3 Parallel trenches made 16–18 July.
4 Boyau trenches made 18–19 July, battery of
   four guns and one howitzer from 26 July.
5 Boyau trenches made 24–25 July.
6 Grenadier redoubt.
7 Grenadier redan with two guns, four guns
   from 24 July.
8 Coehorn battery. Also called Highlanders'
   redoubt as built by the 78th.
9 Admiral's battery of eight guns (four 32 pdr.
   and two 24 pdr.), 17 July.
10 Two batteries of two guns each, 17 July.
   Built by detachments of the 45th and 58th.
11 Two mortar batteries of two mortars each
   (two of 13 inch, two of 8 inch), 13 July.
12 Marine's battery of five guns and two
   howitzers, 12 July. So-called because the
   marines off HMS *Namur* helped to build and
   man it.
13 Batteries of five guns and four mortars.
   Also encampment for Wolfe's corps.
14 Battery of four guns.
15 Battery of two guns.
16 Battery of two howitzers, 19 June.
17 Battery of twelve mortars (two 13 inch,
   two 8 inch and eight royals), 19 June.
18 Battery of three guns, 19 June.
19 Battery at Lighthouse of eight guns, 25 June.

The British works were surrounded by an outer
line of redoubts, a few of which are seen on this
map, to warn of surprise attacks by raiders.

L...bury in North America taken near the Light House ...e Louisburg ...L'Amerique Sept...
...durant le dernier Siege
Drawn ...t by Cap.t Ince of th ...engraved by P. Canot.

ABOVE **View of Louisbourg during the siege from Lighthouse Point. The lighthouse is prominent and, just behind it, the Island Battery can be seen partly covered with smoke. (Print by P. Cannot, after a sketch by Capt. Ince, 35th Foot)**

RIGHT **Interior of the reconstructed chapel in the King's Bastion. The painting shows Saint-Louis, King Louis IX of France, to whom the chapel was dedicated.**

Almost incredibly, by the evening of the 3rd, the semicircular Grenadier's Redoubt was ready. It was a large work, capable of holding up to 500 men. British batteries were built near Grenadier's Redoubt at the same time, and in the following days various improvements were made at Green Hill. The French artillery fire from the city and the ships continued to be very heavy. A British battery with some 17 "Royal" and "Cohorn" mortars near the Grenadier's Redoubt opened fire on the town.

In the evening, the British started bombarding the French ships with hot shot; the Marquis Desgouttes ordered that only 50 men remain on each ship in case the ships caught fire and exploded. The seamen were sent to serve the guns and repair the works in the bastions, while the marines joined the garrison. The British fire ceased when it became too dark, especially as there was much fog.

4 July The French noted the arrival of more cannon, and work progressing in several places on the nearby hills, while "the cannonading continued (but not much) from the town" and from the French ships according to Amherst. The new mortar battery at Green Hill fired on the French ships. The British were certainly busy, with many hundreds of men toiling to put up field works and make fascines. These were not cannon-proof, but covered hundreds of men "not exposed to [the] sight" of the French. The four grenadier companies posted to protect the forward redoubt were very exposed, so Wolfe withdrew all but one company of grenadiers to cover behind the nearby hills.

French iron 12-in. mortar with its iron bed. This was one of several iron mortars cast for the French Navy in 1756 and now at the Canadian War Museum, Ottawa. The British referred to these as "13 inch" mortars as the old French measure was slightly longer than the British.

Unknown to the British, the French planned a sortie that night with 800 men including the five volunteer companies, a grenadier company and various piquets under Lt. Col. d'Anthonay. At midnight, the troops were assembled and were about to go out, but the sortie was canceled when French scouts reported that many British troops were nearby.

5 July It was a "very rainy bad day" according to Amherst; foggy and rainy weather until about noon according to Drucour. Amherst noted that an "immense number of fascines" were "swallowed up" in the muddy ground, "for want of being properly drained", while Drucour's guns, including two 6-pdrs. at Black Rock Point, shot at the British works under construction in the afternoon. In the harbor, some of the French ships moved closer to bombard Grenadier's Redoubt and the nearby batteries.

6 July Another battery near Grenadier's Redoubt now opened fire specifically on the French ships with their four 12-pdr. cannons. It was joined by other batteries in the nearby hills and the mortar battery. The cannonade exchange was very heavy during the whole day. Every once in a while, the British would also fire mortar shells, which burst into Louisbourg. Amherst visited all the works during the day and asked Admiral Boscawen to send four 32-pdrs. for Wolfe's batteries, "to which he readily agreed."

The Marquis Desgouttes permanently landed most of the sailors and marines from his ship to serve in town. The sailors went to serve as gunners in the La Grave Battery, while the sea-soldiers joined the other marines already landed and formed into a temporary corps under M. Datehou to serve with the town's garrison.

In the evening, one of the British batteries managed to enfilade the frigate *L'Aréthuse,* "whose Fire had done so much mischief in retarding the Works on the right and killing many men at the Epaulement" (Gordon), and it withdrew nearer to the town. This meant that the British siege works between Green Hill and the town would be much safer. The British batteries concentrated their fire mostly on the ships in the harbor during 6 and 7 July.

On the outskirts, Boishébert reported that some of his men burned a house and killed a sentry at the British army's outer perimeter during the night.

7 July The morning was very foggy. Wolfe's proposal to build another large battery and install the 32-pdr. cannons with which he hoped to ruin the Dauphin and the King's bastions was approved by Amherst. Elsewhere, there was a good deal of skirmishing between the French and British advanced posts.

By now, the British bombardment of the town was regular. The women and children, with other civilians unable to bear arms, were huddled into the town's casemates as these were the safest places. The British gunners tried to avoid the town's hospital, easily plotted because of its chapel's spire, although it was on the trajectory of guns firing on the eastern part of the town's fortifications. As the hospital overflowed, a field hospital was set up under tents, and was also exposed to the fire of British guns. Drucour sent a drummer under a flag of truce with a letter about this, but nothing was formally resolved. Amherst felt it would also protect the French main powder magazine. As for the able French soldiers, they were "borne down with fatigue" and preferred sleeping in

MADAME DRUCOUR FIRES THE GUNS, JUNE–JULY 1758

One of the most energetic and engaging figures in the French garrison of Louisbourg was the wife of the governor. It was observed that "this lady performed, during the siege, actions which will insure her a place amongst the illustrious persons of her sex; she fired herself three cannons every day to encourage the artillerymen." General Amherst too was impressed by her bravery during the siege and this led to a charming episode of the "lace wars" in the New World. During a truce, Amherst had two pineapples, then a rare delicacy, sent to her as a present. Madame de Drucour returned the courtesy by sending him bottles of wine, and went on firing her three cannons a day. The scene of the painting occurs in the Dauphin Bastion with Madame de Drucour in a green dress and white cape-shawl

P. Courcelle

holding a portfire stick, helped by an officer of the colonial artillery. An accompanying lady-in-waiting stands near a corporal, distinguished by the silver lace edging his cuffs. The scene shown would be typical of all French batteries in Louisbourg which were served by *Canonniers-Bombardiers* colonial gunners and sailor-gunners landed from the trapped French warships in the harbour. The French ordnance in Louisbourg consisted of iron naval guns.

the streets where they were only exposed to shells rather than in their barracks where they could be killed by both shot and shell.

8 July There was little firing during the night as a heavy rain fell until 7 am and it was a relatively quiet day thereafter. The British continued work on their batteries, the French engineers made plans to reinforce the Queen's Battery and to build a battery holding four 12-pdrs. at Black Rock Point which might halt the progress of the British on that side. At 9 pm, Drucour and his officers decided to make a sortie during the night.

THE FRENCH SORTIE

9 July Between 1 am and 2 am, the French made a sortie to the west of the town. Their force consisted of two companies of grenadiers, the five companies of volunteers and six picquets, totaling about 720 men under Lt. Col. Marin of the Bourgogne Regiment. They were divided into two columns and moved in the dark until they came up to a working party that they captured, then moved against the first British advanced post. It seems that most of the British grenadiers of Forbes' 17th Foot were asleep. The French attacked at bayonet point and carried the advanced post, killing Lord Dundonald, captain of the grenadiers, with another grenadier and wounding 16. Some of the British soldiers managed to escape to the second line to give the alarm, but were closely followed by French soldiers. In the British camp, the drums were beating the general alarm and it was clear to Marin and his men that they would not get much further.

Workmen who followed the French soldiers set about demolishing the works. There was not much time. A detachment of Whitmore's 22nd was advancing with others following, putting pressure on the French. After destroying what they could, the French returned to the city, taking with them two captured British officers and 28 grenadiers. The British suffered five killed, 29 wounded or missing and the two officers taken, according to Amherst, while the French had two officers and 28 men killed, four officers and 21 men wounded, according to Grésigny. However the accounts differ on details and casualties regarding this sortie. An anonymous French naval officer's journal (appended to Capt. John Montresor's diary) mentions that the sortie was "so badly conducted that our soldiers fired on each other by which we lost more men than the enemy." This would have likely occurred in the confusion of the retreat back into town. Some British accounts, including Amherst's, say the French were "drunk." This may have been due to the hefty ration of brandy issued to the men before going out, a common practice in armies before an action, although it is not mentioned in French diaries. There was "continual fire from the town during the time of the sortie," according to William Amherst.

Grenadier, Forbes' 17th Foot, 1750s. The 17th's grenadiers were surprised by the French sortie on 9 July, which killed their captain, Lord Dundonald, and part of the company. (Print after D. Morier)

After a truce to bury the dead, the artillery duels continued through the day, with the French ships targeting particularly Wolfe's batteries on the west side of town. In the evening, the British started building a six-gun battery near Grenadier's Redoubt.

10 July At about 1 am, all the British outer guard posts were alerted by several fires in the nearby woods, started by Boishébert's party of irregulars, but nothing further occurred. The British rear was well secured against incursions by a network of outer redans and redoubts, with strong detachments guarding them and companies of rangers patrolling the area.

The British trench to the west of the town, dug between the harbor and Green Hill, was now just about completed and the epaulement on the covert-way was easier to build thanks to proper drainage. Later that day, some 200 British miners, recruited from the crews of Admiral Boscawen's warships, joined the army on land. The French fired many shells at the British but, noted Amherst, "all without effect." However, the French ships knocked out two British guns in Wolfe's batteries.

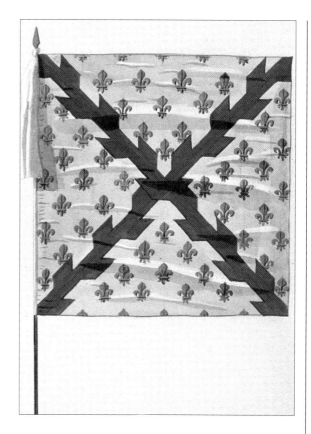

ARTILLERY DUELS

11 July The French ships and town batteries opened up intense fire on the new six-gun battery. Wolfe's request for seven more 24-pdrs. was acted upon, and two additional 32-pdrs. were also landed from Boscawen's ships. Still, the French fire was very heavy and, among the casualties was Col. Bastide, who was laid up by a contusion caused by a musket ball which hit him on the thickest part of his boot. Drucour gleefully noted that the ships caused considerable damage to the new battery, which would have to be rebuilt during the night.

On the outskirts of the British camp, Boishébert's Indians captured a wagoner to question him for information. He managed to escape the next day and reported to Amherst that he had seen about 250 Canadians – some were actually Acadians – and 12 Indians about four miles into the woods. In fact, Boishébert's forces were diminishing fast. His Acadian militiamen from Port Toulouse mostly deserted, as did all the Indians; over 50 men were sick and he reported having only 140 men left by mid-July.

12–13 July From midnight to about 9 am, it rained heavily and intermittently for most of the day. Visibility was poor so there was less shooting from either side. A shelter was built about 250 meters in front of Green Hill during the night. The work on the six-gun battery continued under French fire. The next day, the French fire slackened considerably, probably because of the rain. Their new work to cover Black Rock Point was progressing. Meanwhile, to the west, the new six-gun British battery was completed and opened fire on the Dauphin Bastion and its cavalier.

Battalion color, Bourgogne Infantry Regiment, c. 1744–75. This regiment, along with Royal-Comtois, was allowed to have the ragged red saltire Burgundy Cross in its battalion colors rather than the white cross seen in French infantry colors. (Anne S. K. Brown Military Collection. Brown University)

GENERAL AMHERST AT A BRITISH BATTERY, JULY 1758

As the British forces secured positions that enclosed the town and the harbor of Louisbourg, General Amherst made sure that logistics for large and substantial batteries would be available to bombard the city and the ships in the harbor. In spite of persistent difficulties due to the weather, this was accomplished largely thanks to the efforts of Admiral Boscawen's Royal Navy officers and sailors. In this respect, given the complexity of the operation, one of the first of this scale to be attempted by British forces, it stands as a model of what can be achieved by harmonious relations between the army and the navy. Amherst was not a tactical genius but he was outstanding at using carefully and methodically all resources at hand and keeping good relations with senior officers. He is shown accompanied by several officers inspecting a battery of heavy siege guns manned by personnel of the Royal Artillery. Our rendition is largely after David Morrier and a plate showing the batteries by Thomas Davies, a Royal Artillery officer who was present at the siege. There was no cavalry but some horses would have been available to British senior officers and for transport. Amherst is taken after a portrait by Sir Joshua Reynolds showing a relatively plain coat with blue lapels and gold lace, probably his favored campaign dress.

14 July The weather was better but it was very windy with a "vast surf" which did not prevent the renewal of a vigorous artillery duel. A new British battery of two guns was begun near the six-gun battery at the Grenadier's Redoubt. Built by men of the 45th Foot, it was called Warburton's Battery. On the British right, the siege works were slowly approaching the city, and two new batteries, one of six guns and one of eight, were started.

15 July The new French work at Black Rock Point was completed and mounted two 12-pdrs. Although the weather was again very bad, Amherst reconnoitered the positions to the west of the town and doubled the number of men in the area. The number of men camping further back was the same as the number of troops posted in the trenches between the harbor and Green Hill. This reduced the amount of marching needed, as they could quickly support each other if attacked.

Since 9 July, the British had concentrated part of their fire on the ships in the harbor, damaging their masts, riggings and hulls. During the night, the frigate *L'Aréthuse* managed to slip out of the harbor. She was spotted by the British at Lighthouse Point who fired rockets to warn the fleet of her departure. The Lighthouse battery fired at her in the dark and Sir Charles Hardy's squadron answered the rocket signals and gave chase, but the wily and lucky Captain Vauquelin slipped through and got away, the last French ship to leave Louisbourg.

16 July An hour before dawn, a party of about 100 Canadians and Indians attacked one of the British guard posts at the northeast end of

An iron 24-pdr. French marine artillery cannon mounted on the King's Bastion. The guns in Louisbourg were naval models from the French navy. Most were probably the 1703 model, which remained in general use until 1766.

Cannon mounted on the King's Bastion. This bastion's guns covered the area south of the town.

the harbor, but it was well fortified and they withdrew. There was much firing and excitement in the British camp; Wolfe's grenadiers and 170 of Scott's light infantry went after them but they had already vanished. Another party of about "50 savages" was seen at the head of Gabarus Bay. Amherst sent 100 men after them, but they too vanished.

In the evening Wolfe ordered Lt. Browne with 20 rangers and Lt. Gore with 20 grenadiers of the 35th Foot to capture a French advanced post at Barachois (or Barasoi), only 250 meters from the Dauphin Gate. They did so briskly and the French volunteers retired into the city while Wolfe immediately sent in reinforcements. Within minutes, four companies of grenadiers, three of the 78th, and a detachment of the 58th were on the spot and entrenching themselves to secure that position, as well as two nearby hills to their right. The French fired a hail of bullets and grapeshot from the ramparts but did not hit much in the dark. By morning, the British had dug enough to have good cover.

17 July The British continued to bombard the ships in the harbor and strengthen their positions around the city. However, the French certainly responded, as Amherst noted that "the firing continued very great from the town" and the French ships. The artillery duel was "without intermission" and "extremely hot" according to both Maj. Gordon and Drucour. Amherst went to Barachois with Capt. MacKellar of the engineers to "see what could be done to take all the advantages" from it. A communications entrenchment was started to reach the parallel in front of Green Hill, as well as a mortar battery. It was most dangerous work, and an officer of the 1st Foot and several enlisted men were killed, others wounded by the French fire.

LEFT **Private, Artois Infantry Regiment, *c.* 1757. (Musée de l'Armée, Paris)**

OPPOSITE RIGHT **Private, Grenadier Company, Webb's 48th Foot, 1750s. Grenadiers were distinguished by their pointed and decorated miter caps, and the wings at the end of each shoulder. Uniforms were not altered and remained as they would have been in Europe during the Louisbourg campaign. This soldier is shown with his knapsack slung over the left shoulder, his haversack slung plainly visible over his right shoulder, with his tin water canteen. The white gaiters were replaced by brown "marching" gaiters on campaign. (Anne S. K. Brown Military Collection. Brown University)**

18 July Work continued on strengthening the British entrenchments. The parapet was made cannon-proof and the work on a parallel trench was progressed briskly. Although the French fired constantly, the British in the trenches were relatively lucky, having only 11 killed and 30 wounded in the previous 48 hours. Meanwhile, the British batteries on the west side of the city at White Point were getting stronger and more effective. Their main target was now the Dauphin Bastion's cavalier and the spur.

19 July The furious artillery duel continued, but on the west side, the British were gaining the upper hand. They managed to enfilade an end of the cavalier on the Dauphin Bastion, and British fire destroyed the carriages of two French guns. Amherst sent fresh battalions to relieve the men in the trenches.

20 July The Dauphin Bastion's spur was reduced to silence and its cavalier was seriously damaged with several embrasures destroyed. The damage to the bastion was severe and the British reported that its fire considerably slackened. Work on the British parallel went on and some 400 sailors were landed to help at the works on the British right. At night, however, the French made repairs and opened up "a great fire" from the Dauphin Bastion, enough, according to Amherst, "to have destroyed the whole army," but the British were lucky and casualties were light.

LOSS OF THREE FRENCH SHIPS

21 July At 2 pm the British gunners firing at the French ships had a great stroke of luck. One of their mortar shells squarely hit the poop deck of *L'Entreprenant,* setting fire to the ship. It was impossible to put out, and the flames spread to *Le Célèbre* and *Le Capricieux. L'Entreprenant* blew up and the two other ships were almost totally consumed by 7 pm.

It was a heavy loss for the French, and Wolfe's batteries could now fire almost unhindered by the warships. Bombardment of the Dauphin Bastion was accordingly very heavy, and embrasures were badly damaged. Drucour noted that its cavalier was so weakened that it could crumble at any time.

22 July Two new British batteries south of town consisting of 13 24-pdr. cannons and seven mortar went into action and fired "with great success" on the Queen's Bastion according to Amherst, who also noted that the French gunners "likewise fired very well on them and threw their shells extremely well." There followed a curious incident as a French "shot went just into the muzzle of a [British] 24-pdr. and stuck there as if it had been forged to be rammed in." A British battery of four 24-pdr. guns was started on the left side of the King's Bastion. All these British bombardments finally set on fire the large building housing the barracks, the chapel and the governor's quarters which the British called the citadel. There were also fires in the town, so part of the garrison was occupied with fire-fighting. Many French guns in batteries all over the town were knocked out of action.

23 July On the British left, a second parallel was started, which crept ever closer to the Dauphin Bastion, while a small redoubt was begun on the right. Again, the British gunnery was

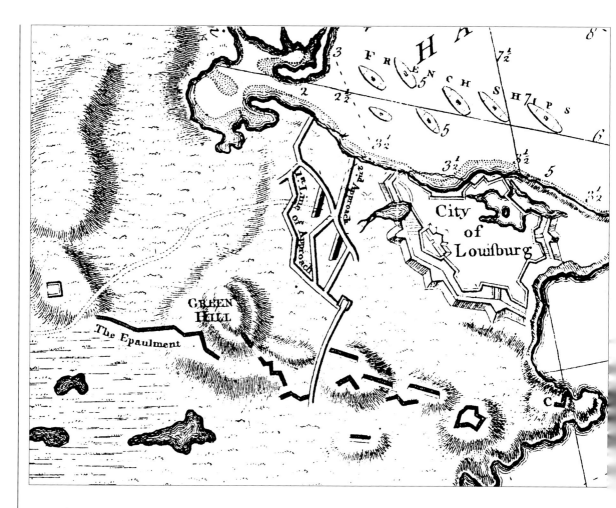

The final stages of the siege, 25–26 July. The British parallel trenches in the north were a few dozen yards from the Dauphin Gate, and the Dauphin Bastion has a noticeably large breach. The many black bars are British batteries. (Detail from Jefferey's map)

very effective, starting many fires in the town. Col. Bastide, the chief engineer who had been wounded on the 8th, was now well enough to mount a horse and resume his duties. Some 400 sailors finished the battery to the left of the King's Bastion. At 10 pm, the wooden barracks originally built by the British and New Englanders in 1745–46 went up in flames "which we had not have better done" reflected Amherst, no doubt already wondering how he would lodge his troops once the town surrendered.

24 July After inspecting the Dauphin Bastion at dawn, Drucour concluded that it would "soon be out of use," and that the French batteries were generally "in a sad state." The British continued to pour a heavy fire into the town and "silenced the guns" in the Queen's Bastion. The British battery on the right side of the King's Bastion was completed and opened fire in the afternoon. Admiral Boscawen sent ashore another 400 sailors to carry ammunition and supplies. Another battery containing five guns was started next to the four-gun battery at the left of the King's Bastion. The admiral also sent ashore another 200 miners who, joined to the 100 already with the army, made a corps of 300; half of them worked on the trenches. The French maintained a heavy fire against them, but the British were now so close that they could fire muskets "into the Embrazures [and] beat them off their guns" (Amherst).

FRENCH WALLS BREACHED AND LAST SHIPS LOST

25 July The British batteries again "played with great success" on their various targets. The fortifications were crumbling faster than they could be repaired. Col. Franquet reported a breach in the Dauphin Bastion. William Amherst, who was in the British trenches, reported that a trench had advanced to within 50 meters of the glacis of the Dauphin Bastion. Scaling ladders were sent to the trenches in preparation for an assault.

By now, the town offered a pitiful sight. Many of its buildings were burned and others partly demolished by the intense bombardments of the last few weeks. There was hardly a structure which did not have pieces of shells or cannonballs embedded in its walls. The town's population was shell-shocked, having been traumatized by the intense bombardments and huddled in casemates every day and night for weeks on end.

26 July Admiral Boscawen advised Amherst that he had selected captains John Laforey and George Balfour to lead 600 sailors and marines into the harbor in longboats during the night to attack the two remaining French warships. Amherst went to the trenches and, after midnight, "began to despair of the boats coming." They finally arrived at about 1.30 am under the cover of a fog. The 74-gun *Prudent* was attacked

Captains Laforey and Balfour's attack with sailors and marines on *Le Prudent* and *Le Bienfaisant* in Louisbourg harbor on the night of 25–26 July 1758. *Le Prudent* ran aground and was set on fire, while *Le Bienfaisant* was captured. (Print after Richard Paton)

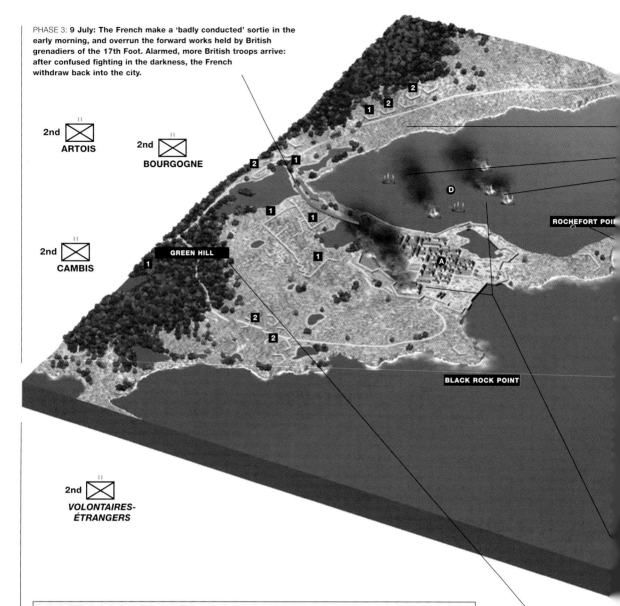

PHASE 3: **9 July: The French make a 'badly conducted' sortie in the early morning, and overrun the forward works held by British grenadiers of the 17th Foot. Alarmed, more British troops arrive: after confused fighting in the darkness, the French withdraw back into the city.**

2nd ⊠ **ARTOIS**

2nd ⊠ **BOURGOGNE**

2nd ⊠ **CAMBIS**

2nd ⊠ *VOLONTAIRES-ÉTRANGERS*

GREEN HILL

ROCHEFORT POI

BLACK ROCK POINT

PHASE 1: **26 June: British troops occupy Green Hill: this becomes their focus point for the siege works to be advanced from the west and north-west side of town. Stiff resistance by the French makes the construction of field fortifications very slow and hazardous and, at times, impossible in the following days.**

FRENCH UNITS

A Artois Regiment, 2nd Bn.
  Bourgogne Regiment, 2nd Bn.
  Cambis Regiment, 2nd Bn.
  Volontaires-Étrangers Regiment, 2nd Bn.
  Compagnies franches de la Marine (colonial infantry).
  Canonniers-Bombardiers (colonial artillery).
  Bourgeois Militia.
  Compagnies franches de la Marine (metropolitan marines detached from ships).
  Sailors from French ships, part served as gunners in Louisbourg's batteries.

B *L'Apollon* 50 guns, scuttled 28–29 June.
  Le Fidèle 36 guns, scuttled 28–29 June.
  La Chèvre 16 guns, scuttled 28–29 June.
  La Biche 16 guns, scuttled 28–29 June.

C (not shown)
  L'Aréthuse 36 guns, escaped 15 July.

D *L'Entreprenant* 74 guns, burnt 21 July.
  Le Capricieux 64 guns, burnt 21 July.
  Le Célèbre 64 guns, burnt 21 July.
  Le Prudent 74 guns, burnt 26 July.
  Le Bienfaisant 64 guns, taken 26 July.

BRITISH UNITS

1 1st Foot, 2nd Bn (Royal Scots).
  15th Foot (Amhert's).
  17th Foot (Forbes').
  22nd Foot (Whitmore's).
  28th Foot (Bragg's).
  35th Foot (Otway's).
  40th Foot (Hopson's).
  45th Foot (Warburton's).
  47th Foot (Lascelles').
  48th Foot (Webb's).
  58th Foot (Anstruther's).
  60th Foot, 2nd Bn (Lawrence's).
  60th Foot, 3rd Bn (Monckton's).
  78th Foot (Fraser's Highlanders).

2 Royal Artillery and sailors detached from the British ships.

3 Royal Navy ships blockade the harbor.

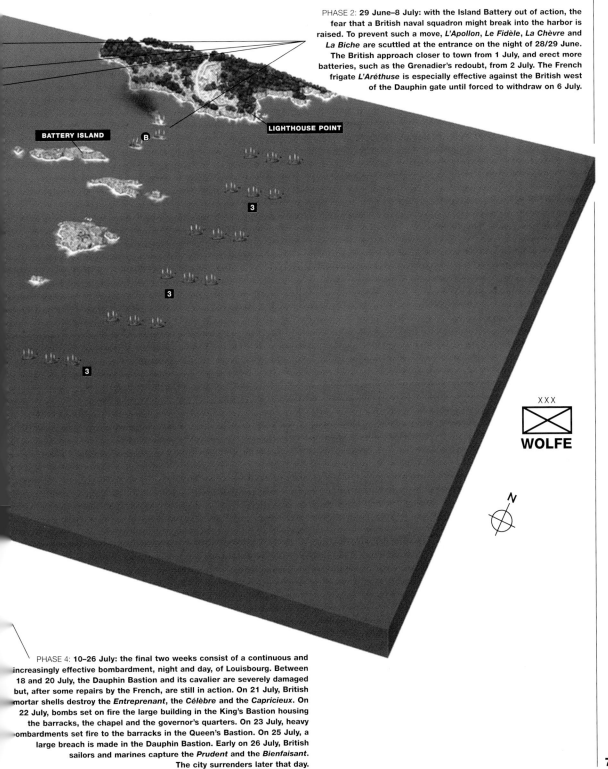

PHASE 2: **29 June–8 July:** with the Island Battery out of action, the fear that a British naval squadron might break into the harbor is raised. To prevent such a move, *L'Apollon*, *Le Fidèle*, *La Chèvre* and *La Biche* are scuttled at the entrance on the night of 28/29 June. The British approach closer to town from 1 July, and erect more batteries, such as the Grenadier's redoubt, from 2 July. The French frigate *L'Aréthuse* is especially effective against the British west of the Dauphin gate until forced to withdraw on 6 July.

BATTERY ISLAND

B

LIGHTHOUSE POINT

3

3

3

XXX

WOLFE

N

PHASE 4: **10–26 July:** the final two weeks consist of a continuous and increasingly effective bombardment, night and day, of Louisbourg. Between 18 and 20 July, the Dauphin Bastion and its cavalier are severely damaged but, after some repairs by the French, are still in action. On 21 July, British mortar shells destroy the *Entreprenant*, the *Célèbre* and the *Capricieux*. On 22 July, bombs set on fire the large building in the King's Bastion housing the barracks, the chapel and the governor's quarters. On 23 July, heavy bombardments set fire to the barracks in the Queen's Bastion. On 25 July, a large breach is made in the Dauphin Bastion. Early on 26 July, British sailors and marines capture the *Prudent* and the *Bienfaisant*. The city surrenders later that day.

first by British sailors "armed with cutlass, pistol & hatchet" (William Amherst). According to Drucour, one of its officers had ordered the head gunner to set it on fire should the ship be in danger of being taken, but he was not sure if it was him or the British sailors that had set the ship alight when it ran aground. *Le Prudent* was certainly doomed to go up in flames and it soon did. British sailors and marines also boarded and captured the 64-gun *Bienfaisant* and quickly towed it to the other end of the harbor. Boscawen was elated and now planned to force the harbor's entrance with six of his warships.

By the time the sun rose, the day had already been disastrous for the garrison of Louisbourg. The capture of the ships was the *coup de grâce* for the defenders' morale. The bombardments had caused a breach in the Dauphin Bastion and another would soon be apparent in the King's Bastion. Of the 52 cannons opposed to the British batteries, 40 had been knocked out of action. Drucour bowed to the inevitable and sent a message to Amherst proposing terms for a capitulation.

THE CAPITULATION

At 8 am on 26 July, Boishébert noted that the cannon fire constantly heard in the distance for weeks, night and day, had ceased. Negotiations were under way and the French garrison hoped to obtain the "honors of war" as had been granted to the British garrison at Minorca. That would have meant they could keep their personal weapons and their colors, and be transported back to France, retaining their honor as soldiers. Amherst and Boscawen answered that the garrison was to surrender as prisoners-of-war; there would be no honors, and the French had an hour to comply. In retrospect, such terms seem unusually harsh against an obviously valiant garrison, especially in an age when battles were conducted by officers who usually behaved with the gallantry expected of gentlemen.

The conditions imposed by Amherst insulted Drucour and his senior officers. After such a valiant defense they felt they and their men deserved the honors of war. Drucour asked for better terms, but Amherst was adamant. Mortified, Drucour and his officers resolved to die fighting in the town's rubble. Col. Franquet had already chosen the Princess Bastion as the best place for a last stand. Present at the senior officer's war council was Commissaire-Ordonnateur Prévost, who begged the military officers to reconsider. Their sacrifice would not alter the military outcome of the siege, but it would put the civilians and wounded at great risk. In the event of a general assault, all control is often lost of the battle- and blood-crazed soldiers, and civilians, women in particular, were likely to suffer the worst outrages if they were not massacred outright. Their

RIGHT **Captain George B. Rodney commanded the 74-gun HMS *Dublin* at Louisbourg. He achieved flag rank and gained lasting fame from his victory at the battle of the Saints in 1782.**

LEFT **Color bearer, Cambis Regiment, _c._ 1755–62. The second battalion's colors were seized and burned by the men when they learned Gen. Amherst had not granted the "honors of war" to the garrison in spite of its valiant defense. (Fortress Louisbourg National Historic Site, Louisbourg, Nova Scotia)**

first duty was to afford some protection to the civilians and the weak, Prévost argued, rather than save their pride. Bowing to this inexorable logic, they reluctantly agreed except for the commanders of the Artois, Bourgogne, and Cambis regiments. Drucour sent word to Amherst that the garrison would surrender on his terms.

If the civilians were relieved and some of the soldiers pleased they had at least survived the ordeal, others were not as gleeful. Resentment was especially acute in the Cambis Regiment. The men, outraged at having to surrender their muskets and the battalion's colors to the hated British, mutinied, broke their muskets, seized the colors and burned them. The other troops were calmer. Some looting was reported and it was rumored that some money was stolen by _Volontaires-Étrangers_ officers. Some French officers even feared that the British might take revenge for the Indian attack on the prisoners at Fort William-Henry the preceding year.

On the morning of 27 July, the three senior British grenadier companies took over the Dauphin Gate from the French sentries. At 12 noon, wrote Amherst, the "Garrison lay down their arms" and its 11 remaining colors. Some 221 cannons and 18 mortars were found in the town.

In terms of casualties, the French reported 102 killed and 303 wounded of their land forces at the time of the surrender, a total of 405. The British reported 172 killed and 355 wounded of their land forces, a total of 527. These figures vary little from one account to the other. Most of the casualties occurred during the daily artillery duels and the French gunners did remarkably well under adverse circumstances. There were more losses among sailors, marines and civilians on both sides but no figures are given of their casualties, except that the French had 1,347 sailors and marines sick and wounded on 26 July. Overall, it would appear that the French inflicted five casualties to every four they sustained.

While the siege of Louisbourg was going on, the battle of Ticonderoga was fought on 8 July, when, Gen. Abercromby's large British and American army was defeated by Gen. Montcalm's far

BRITISH SAILORS BOARDING *LE BIENFAISANT*, 26 JULY 1758

In the early morning hours of 26 July, some 600 Royal Navy sailors and marines under captains John Laforey and George Balfour sneaked up to the two remaining French warships in Louisbourg harbor, the 74-gun *Prudent* and the 64-gun *Bienfaisant*. Wielding pistols, sabers, and hatchets, they boarded both ships and overcame their skeleton crews - most of the French sailors and marines had long been landed to serve in the city - after some resistance. Our plate shows Royal Navy sailors led by an officer boarding *Le Bienfaisant* from their longboats and overcoming French sailors on watch except one, who sounds the alarm with his whistle. *Le Prudent*, which had meanwhile caught on fire, is seen in the background. *Le Bienfaisant* was captured and towed away. This was a most discouraging blow to the garrison and, with the Dauphin Bastion now breached, the city surrendered later that day.

smaller French force. The French defenders in Ticonderoga and Louisbourg were not in positions where they could maneuver. The detailed reasons for Abercromby's failure are given in *Campaign 76: Ticonderoga 1758* (Oxford, Osprey, 2000) by the same author, and the differences with Amherst's conduct of the campaign at Louisbourg are striking. The patient and methodical Amherst used every advantage at his disposal and wasted none of them; he used his subordinates to the best of their varied talents; he never lost control of the operations and his relations with Admiral Boscawen were exemplary. Amherst was not a brilliant tactician with a genius for battlefield moves like Marlborough or Frederick the Great; he always enjoyed superior numbers to his enemies in all his campaigns and his great quality was that he never wasted that superiority.

Upon receiving the news of the fall of Louisbourg, some in Quebec expected the British to attack the capital of New France by late August. In fact, it was already too late in the year to mount such an expedition because of the difficult sailing conditions of the St Lawrence River and the short season of good weather. As Phipp's failed 1690 expedition had shown, being late to attack Quebec could have disastrous results (see *Osprey Military Journal*, Vol. 1, Issue 2). As it was, Montcalm's incredible victory at Ticonderoga against Abercromby's army, and Drucour's stubborn resistance until the end of July had given Canada another year under the French flag.

The strategic results of Louisbourg's capitulation, added to the results of the year's campaign on other fronts, were later clearly summed up by the Marquis de Vaudreuil, governor-general of New France. "The British," he wrote to the French court, "are masters of Louisbourg, are holding Gaspé, are at the bottom of Lake George, are perhaps master of the Ohio," and have thus surrounded Canada from all sides. They could now attack "from four sides: at Quebec, at Lake Ontario, at the Ohio and at Lake Champlain" against which the French could only oppose 3,500 metropolitan troops, 1,500 colonial regular troops, and 8,000 embodied militiamen (AC, C11A, Vol. 103). The continued support of the Indians was rightly considered tenuous at best; food and various equipment were in short supply. With the Royal Navy controlling the Gulf of St Lawrence, substantial relief from France was considered very unlikely. New France was doomed.

Maj. Roger Morris (1717–94). Morris' first experience of warfare in America was as ADC to Gen. Braddock in the disastrous Monongahela expedition of 1755. He was in command of troops at Lighthouse Point in July at the siege of Louisbourg. He also served in the expedition up the St John River with Monkton after the siege, and was with Wolfe at Quebec the following year. He served with the 35th Foot in 1758 but later transferred to the 47th, in whose uniform he is shown in this *c.* 1760 miniature. (New Brunswick Museum)

AFTERMATH

SECURING ATLANTIC CANADA

Once in possession of Louisbourg, Amherst wished to consolidate his position. He began by sending the French garrison and Louisbourg's civilian population back to Europe in August.

As Isle Saint-Jean was included in the capitulation of Louisbourg, Lt. Col. Lord Rollo was sent in August with 300 men detached from the 22nd, 28th, 40th, and 45th regiments, 200 light infantrymen, and Capt. James Rogers' Rangers. As in Nova Scotia three years earlier, the island's Acadian population was to be deported and their dwellings destroyed. The sad scenes of desolation, broken families and burned homes were thus repeated during the summer and early fall. Over 2,400 Acadians were reported embarked for France by November, never to see their garden island again.

Now enjoying total naval control of the area, Boscawen and Amherst quickly resolved to send a squadron with a strong contingent of troops to the Gaspé Peninsula, where there were a number of French fishing

View of the Miramichi River with the small French settlement at the left, 1758. (print after Capt. Hervey Smyth)

establishments that could supply Acadian partisans, some of whom operated from schooners and other small craft. All these establishments were to be razed. Sir Charles Hardy sailed from Louisbourg on 29 August with eight warships and six transports carrying the 15th, 28th, and 58th regiments under Wolfe's command. The force arrived at Gaspé Bay on 4 September. As there were no French military forces in the area, the troops landed unopposed, rounded up anybody they found, leveled to the ground whatever stood, and sank fishing boats. These actions were repeated further to the south-west of the peninsula's coast at Grande-Rivière, and Pabos. But Wolfe wished to strike much closer to the St Lawrence, and sent Maj. Dalling with some 300 men by land from Gaspé Bay to Mont-Louis, on top of the peninsula, at about 150 kms east of Matane. After a difficult five-day march edging the shore, they reached Mont-Louis on 19 September, razed the place and came back, manning the boats seized there. Some fishermen and their families escaped into the woods, but hundreds were rounded up by the British and deported to France.

Wolfe sent another party under Col. James Murray, commanding the 15th and part of the 28th, as far south as Miramichi with orders to

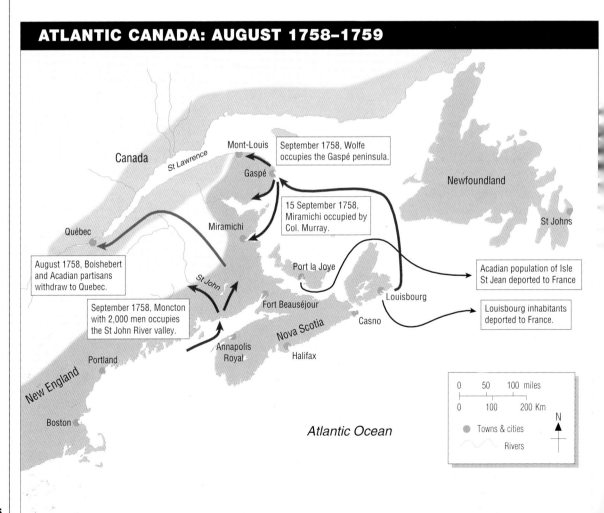

ATLANTIC CANADA: AUGUST 1758–1759

Canada

Newfoundland

St Lawrence

Mont-Louis

September 1758, Wolfe occupies the Gaspé peninsula.

Gaspé

15 September 1758, Miramichi occupied by Col. Murray.

Québec

Miramichi

St Johns

August 1758, Boishebert and Acadian partisans withdraw to Quebec.

St John

Port la Joye

Acadian population of Isle St Jean deported to France.

September 1758, Moncton with 2,000 men occupies the St John River valley.

Fort Beauséjour

Louisbourg

Louisbourg inhabitants deported to France.

Nova Scotia

Casno

New England

Portland

Annapolis Royal

Halifax

Boston

Atlantic Ocean

| 0 | 50 | 100 miles |
| 0 | 100 | 200 Km |

● Towns & cities

〜〜 Rivers

N

destroy it. This time, some resistance was expected as it was known that Boishébert commanded the area. On 15 September, Murray's force reached the settlement, found it abandoned and razed it. Miramichi, once so vital in the communication line between Quebec and Louisbourg, was now insignificant to the French. Boishébert and his men had abandoned it in mid-August and gone back to Canada.

With Louisbourg fallen, the British were now able to deal with the persistent aggravation from the French and Indian raiding parties based to the west of Nova Scotia. The 35th, the second battalion of the 60th, 350 light infantry and rangers under Maj. Scott, and a detachment of artillery were tasked with occupying the St John River area. The 2,000-man force sailed from Louisbourg on 28 August, stopped in Halifax to pick up supplies and its commander, Brig. Gen. Robert Monkton, and landed at the mouth of the St John River on 20 September, at the site of the modern city of St John, New Brunswick. A fort was immediately built and named Fort Frederick. As the British had exaggerated reports that Boishébert was lurking in the area with hundreds of men, Monkton sent rangers up the river to find them. They traveled some 130 kms up the river without finding the rumored force of 500 men and 200 Indians which was, in fact, imaginary. However, the area was now securely in British hands, and the force spent the rest of the fall burning isolated dwellings and rounding up hapless civilians for deportation. Some Acadian partisans remained hidden, and the hazardous situation in that area was never really resolved until the end of the war in North America.

The 22nd, 28th, 40th, and 45th regiments were left in garrison at Louisbourg with a company of rangers over the winter of 1758–59. In 1759, the 28th and the rangers went to Quebec with Wolfe, along with the grenadier companies of the three other regiments, forming the famous "Louisbourg Grenadiers" during that campaign. The 28th was replaced by Col. Jonathan Bagley's Massachusetts Provincial Regiment.

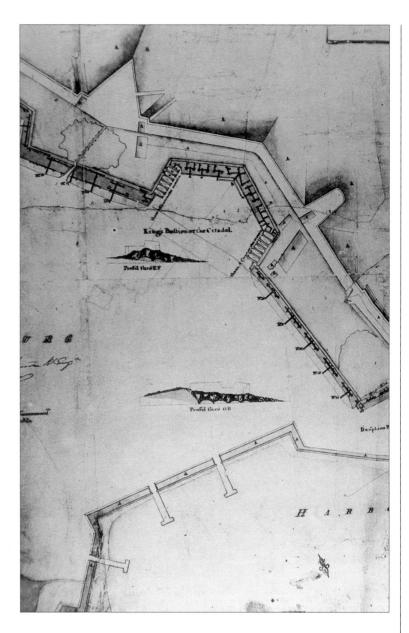

Detail from a British "Plan and Section" of Louisbourg of 1761 showing the fortifications reduced to piles of rubble.

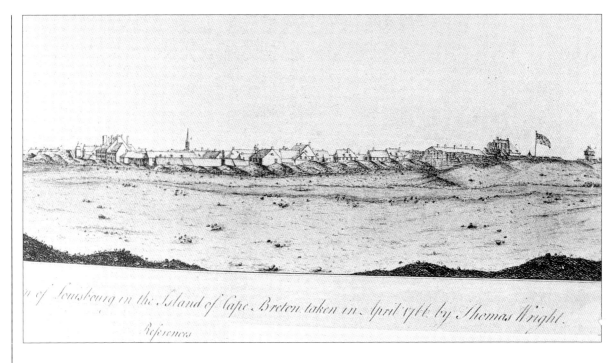

n of Louisbourg in the Island of Cape Breton taken in April 1766 by Thomas Wright.
References

DEMOLITION AND ABANDONMENT

Although the fortress was badly damaged and the town partly in ruins from the 1758 siege, there was still anxiety in Britain and in New England that Louisbourg might be recaptured by the French or, as in 1748, returned to France at the end of the war. True, 1759 had been Britain's "year of victories," but the fortunes of war can be fickle. Thus, in February 1760, it was "His Majesty's orders and Mr. Pitt's," that "all the Fortifications, Works and Deffences whatever shall be totally demolished and Razed." Louisbourg's fortifications proved quite a challenge, and a committee of engineers was consulted. Col. Bastide, who had supervised the 1758 siege operations, was put in charge and arrived at Louisbourg on 24 May 1760 with a company of miners especially raised in England for the purpose, under the command of Capt. De Ruvyne. It was hard work, as Governor Whitmore reported that "the Miners find great difficulty arising from the nature of the earth which however should be surmounted in time," but as they got double pay, they were "pretty well satisfied." So, the summer was spent blowing up all the walls, batteries, and bastions and, by the late fall, all the works had become piles of rubble. Some of the better quarried rocks were taken to Halifax to be used in buildings erected there. With the demolition work done, Col. Bastide and the Company of Miners "sailed from hence the 15th of January [1761] with a fair wind to England" (WO 34/17).

Louisbourg was a fortress no more. The 22nd and most of the 40th and 45th had already left in July 1760 and Bagley's Massachusetts provincials departed for Boston in December. Thereafter, only small detachments of regulars were posted to the town, whose population consisted mostly of dependants from the garrison and various naval establishments. In 1768, its small garrison was withdrawn and what remained of the town's site was eventually abandoned.

Louisbourg in April 1766. All the walls and batteries were now mounds of earth. To the right, the makeshift Fort Frederick with a blockhouse to house the small British garrison, which evacuated in 1768. The spire rising above is that of the hospital. (Print after Thomas Wright)

THE FORTRESS OF LOUISBOURG TODAY

"The Fortress of Louisbourg is to be reconstructed partially so that future generations can thereby see and understand the role of the fortress as a hinge of History. The restoration is to be carried out so that the lessons of History can be animated."

So read the Cabinet Minutes of the Government of Canada in 1961. The economic situation in Cape Breton Island was one of endemic poverty, and in an attempt to offset this, the Canadian federal government decided to develop the economy through tourism. The reconstructed fortress of Louisbourg, in conjunction with the scenic "Cabot Trail" in Cape Breton Highlands National Park, could draw tens of thousands of vacationers to the island. Louisbourg's rebirth was a multi-million-dollar venture that developed over the next two decades. Initially, hardly anyone in government or the museum community knew much about period restorations, conservation criteria, outdoor ecomuseums and the myriad techniques required in the development of large historic sites. Such a major restoration, actually a historic reconstruction, had never been attempted in Canada or anywhere else. An early government objective was to retrain unemployed coal miners in historic construction trades to partially rebuild the town and its fortifications and this was largely achieved. But a credible historic reconstruction also required historians, archeologists, architects, and engineers who had to become specialists in early-18th-century French architecture and colonial life. Somehow, in the years to come, it all came together. Since some features could be reconstructed in several ways, it was finally determined that the date of interpretation would be 1744, just before the first siege.

By 1967–68, the King's Bastion had been reconstructed and, a few years later, the Dauphin Bastion was finished. Although it was not advertised as a

Excavation of timber remains of the drawbridge over the moat leading to the King's Bastion at Louisbourg during the mid-1960s. The drawbridge was nine feet high. (Fortress Louisbourg National Historic Site, Louisbourg, Nova Scotia)

tourist attraction, frequent press reports drew attention to the unusual project and increasing numbers of tourists showed up to visit. By the end of summer 1973, some 140,000 tourists had visited the unfinished site in three months. Reborn, Fortress Louisbourg was now fulfilling its mandate as a major tourist attraction, and has continued to do so; with Cape Breton Highlands National Park, it draws visitors to the eastern end of Nova Scotia in search of natural beauty combined with heritage.

For anyone visiting Fortress Louisbourg today, there is a lot to see. It is probably the best and most accurate reconstruction ever attempted on such a scale. Visitors cross the drawbridge of the Dauphin Gate to find dozens of mid-18th-century buildings. Some, like the Des Gannes house, contain painstaking reconstructions of interiors peopled with costumed animators who seem to know all the 18th-century town gossip. Occasionally, one hears drums announcing drills or a public sale; or even some tumult in the street with tipsy sailors, or a domestic fight (or both!) finally broken up by a squad of soldiers. Some buildings house eating places offering more or less refined 18th-century food, more basic meals are served in a rambling tavern setting. Other houses have displays on the town's life, its buildings, its archeological finds and even its reconstruction.

Outside the fortress walls, there are also many vestiges showing the foundations of destroyed buildings, such as the Royal Battery. If one goes around the harbor and up to Lighthouse Point, the reward is a splendid view of the sea, of the harbor entrance with Battery Island and, in the distance, the fortress town of Louisbourg exactly as it was in the mid-18th century.

RIGHT **Some mid-18th-century Louisbourg gentry chatting with late-20th-century visitors near "L'Epée Royale," the best eating house in the historic town. Those wearing period costumes at Fortress Louisbourg National Historic Site are not re-enactors but historic sites staff and local residents who volunteer their time. All receive training on lifestyles and posture, as well as on Louisbourg's history. The costumes and weapons are carefully made under the supervision of a costume curator; they belong to the site and are only lent to those who have completed the training.**

LEFT The reconstructed Eperon at the Dauphin Gate. A *Canonnier-Bombardier* gunner wearing his red waistcoat and breeches, lounges with an infantryman of the colonial *Compagnies franches* in blue waistcoat and breeches. At the far end of the harbor is the modern town of Louisbourg where visitors can find lodgings, restaurants, and all other conveniences.

RIGHT Soldiers take away a drunken sailor (only visible by his white pants and stockings) to the amusement of visitors at Fortress Louisbourg. This is one of many scenes, always based on actual events found in the archives, that liven up the day.

CHRONOLOGY

1713 Treaty of Utrecht. Acadia and Newfoundland are ceded to Great Britain by France. Summer expedition sails to Isle Royale from France and the settlement of Port St Louis, later renamed Louisbourg, is established.

1715 Louis XV becomes King of France aged five. A Regency Council governs the country.

1719 Louisbourg selected to become the seat of government and the military stronghold of Isle Royale. Initial fortification work begins on the King's Bastion.

1720 Official inauguration of the town as the colony's capital. Commemorative medals are placed in the foundation of the King's Bastion.

1734 Masonry Lighthouse, Canada's first, completed at the harbor entrance.

1736 Lighthouse partially destroyed by fire. Work begins immediately on it's reconstruction.

1743 Fortification works declared completed.

1744 In March war is declared between France and Great Britain. British post at Canso, Nova Scotia, taken by a French force from Louisbourg in May. In December, most of the troops in Louisbourg mutiny, but order is restored.

1745 Louisbourg attacked during May and June by New Englanders, who capture the town on 17 June after a 47-day siege. They deport the majority of the French colonists. Louisbourg occupied by British and New England troops for the next four years.

1746 In July, the small French garrison on Isle Saint-Jean (Prince Edward Island) repulses a New England attack near Port-la-Joie (Charlottetown). During the summer, the Duc d'Anville's expedition aimed at retaking Louisbourg fails.

1748 The War of the Austrian Succession ends with the signing of the Treaty of Aix-la-Chapelle on 18 October. Isle Royale is returned to France.

1749 Louisbourg is reoccupied by the French.

1750 Astronomical observatory is established in the King's Bastion – probably the first in Canada.

1754 Governor Drucour and his wife arrive in Louisbourg on 15 August.

1755 De facto state of war between France and Britain. Both countries send troops to North America. French frontier Forts Beauséjour and Gaspareau captured by Anglo-Americans in June. Acadians deported in the summer and fall resulting in increased raid warfare on Nova Scotia. Work to strengthen and improve the bastions and walls continues in Louisbourg.

1756 War officially declared between France and Great Britain on 18 May. Field works are built at likely landing sites outside the town. British naval squadron near Louisbourg driven off by Beaussier's French squadron.

1757 Failure of British planned expedition to besiege Louisbourg due to presence of French fleet.

1758 Second siege (2 June – 26 July) and capture of Louisbourg. The British deport virtually all the French inhabitants to France.

1760 British destroy Louisbourg's fortifications.

1768 Last British garrison withdrawn from Louisbourg; most of its civilian population also departs.

View of reconstructed Louisbourg in the late 1970s. It is probably the most faithful reconstruction yet attempted thanks to the many excellent plans preserved in the French archives and the painstaking care taken by project construction workers, historians, archeologists, curators, conservators, architects, and administrators. (Fortress Louisbourg National Historic Site, Louisbourg, Nova Scotia)

FURTHER READING

BELOW LEFT **Archeologists, reconstruction architects, and engineers tried to incorporate as many original stones as possible in the rebuilding of Louisbourg. This *c*.1966 photo shows the entrance to a casemate, the recovered stones being numbered and put back into place. Many of the original cut stones came from Rochefort in France and were shipped as ballast to Louisbourg. (Fortress Louisbourg National Historic Site, Louisbourg, Nova Scotia)**

BELOW RIGHT **Bell tower for the Saint-Louis chapel rising above the main building at the King's Bastion. An expert artisan was brought over from France to train Cape Breton Island workers in the tower's reconstruction and intricate slate-cutting work. (Fortress Louisbourg National Historic Site, Louisbourg, Nova Scotia)**

The classic work on Fortress Louisbourg remains John Stewart McLennan's *Louisbourg: From its Foundation to its Fall 1713–1758* (London, 1918 and several reprints). It gives the most complete account of the town's turbulent history and its statistical tables and numerous appendices provide excellent data. The most complete work on the development of the town's fortifications is Bruce W. Fry's *An Appearance of Strength: The Fortifications of Louisbourg* (Ottawa, 1984, 2 vols.). The 1758 siege is mentioned, usually for the length of a chapter, in all the works dealing with the French and Indian War (or Seven Years War) in North America or in biographies of General James Wolfe, but only C. Ochiltree MacDonald's *The Last Siege of Louisbourg* (London, *c.* 1907) appears to have been devoted to the 1758 siege until now. The multi-volume *Dictionary of Canadian Biography* is the standard source for data on the various participants.

Published primary sources are numerous in English concerning the British participants. The most important is *The Journal of Jeffery Amherst … from 1758 to 1763* (J. Clarence Webster, ed., Toronto and Chicago, 1931). See also: G. D. Scull, ed. "The Montresor Journals," *New York Historical*

Society Collections, 1881; Maj. Gordon's journal in *Nova Scotia Historical Society*, 1887; *Journal of William Amherst in America 1758-1760* (J. Clarence Webster, ed., 1927); *The Logs of the Conquest of Canada*, (William Wood, ed., Toronto, 1909); John Knox, *An Historical Journal of the Campaigns in North America* (London, 1769 and many reprints); Northcliffe Collection (Ottawa, 1927) has many useful documents printed as well as a calendar to this outstanding collection.

Documents published in French are few. *Collection de Manuscrits concernant … la Nouvelle-France*, Vol. 4 (Quebec, 1885) has several valuable dispatches and Drucour's summary "*Mémoire*" on the siege; see also Morot de Grésigny's journal in *Revue Historique de L'Armée*, Vol. XXVI (1970), and Boishébert's 1758 journal in the *Bulletin des Recherches Historiques* (Quebec), Vol. XXVII (1921).

Many other documents are unpublished in various archives. In France, Archives Nationales, Colonies (located in Aix), series C11B, Vol. 38 has Drucour's journal of the siege. The Service Historique de L'Armée de Terre, Archives de la Guerre (located at the Château of Vincennes), series A1, Vol. 3457 in particular. Various volumes in Britain's Public Records Office (Kew) in ADM 1, CO 5, WO 1 and WO 34 have British 1758 correspondence (and also a French journal of the siege in WO 34/101). The National (formerly Public) Archives of Canada have various papers and maps relating to the 1758 siege. The research library at Fortress Louisbourg National Historic Site (Louisbourg, Nova Scotia) has copies of unpublished and published works concerning the fortress as well as many specialized unpublished studies on numerous aspects concerning the fortress.

The first building to be reconstructed in the 1960s was also the largest in the town and, indeed, in 18th-century North America. This massive building, which combined official residences, church, and barracks came to about 365 feet long, only 35 feet shorter than the center block of the federal parliament of Canada in Ottawa.

INDEX

Figures in **bold** refer to illustrations

COMPANION SERIES FROM OSPREY

MEN-AT-ARMS

An unrivalled source of information on the organization, uniforms and equipment of the world's fighting men, past and present. The series covers hundreds of subjects spanning 5,000 years of history. Each 48-page book includes concise texts packed with specific information, some 40 photos, maps and diagrams, and eight color plates of uniformed figures.

ELITE

Detailed information on the uniforms and insignia of the world's most famous military forces. Each 64-page book contains some 50 photographs and diagrams, and 12 pages of full-color artwork.

NEW VANGUARD

Comprehensive histories of the design, development and operational use of the world's armored vehicles and artillery. Each 48-page book contains eight pages of full-color artwork including a detailed cutaway.

WARRIOR

Definitive analysis of the armor, weapons, tactics and motivation of the fighting men of history. Each 64-page book contains cutaways and exploded artwork of the warrior's weapons and armor.

ORDER OF BATTLE

The most detailed information ever published on the units that fought history's great battles. Each 96-page book contains comprehensive organization diagrams supported by ultra-detailed color maps. Each title also includes a large fold-out base map.

AIRCRAFT OF THE ACES

Focuses exclusively on the elite pilots of major air campaigns, and includes unique interviews with surviving aces sourced specifically for each volume. Each 96-page volume contains up to 40 specially commissioned artworks, unit listings, new scale plans and the best archival photography available.

COMBAT AIRCRAFT

Technical information from the world's leading aviation writers on the aircraft types flown. Each 96-page volume contains up to 40 specially commissioned artworks, unit listings, new scale plans and the best archival photography available.